GOD'S APPOINTED DESTINY

BE 'TRICE RONIQUE JENKINS DONALD

GOD'S APPOINTED DESTINY

LIFE
A PREPLANNED
DESTINY

"Everything has already been decided. It was known long ago what each person would be. So there's no use arguing with God about your destiny."
—Ecclesiastes 6:10 NLT

TATE PUBLISHING & *Enterprises*

God's Appointed Destiny
Copyright © 2010 by Be 'Trice Ronique Jenkins Donald. All rights reserved.

This title is also available as a Tate Out Loud product. Visit www.tatepublishing.com for more information.

No part of this publication may be reproduced, stored in a retrieval system or transmitted in any way by any means, electronic, mechanical, photocopy, recording or otherwise without the prior permission of the author except as provided by USA copyright law.

Scripture quotations marked (AMP) are taken from the *Amplified Bible*, Copyright © 1954, 1958, 1962, 1964, 1965, 1987 by The Lockman Foundation. Used by permission.

Scripture quotations marked (KJV) are taken from the *Holy Bible, King James Version*, Cambridge, 1769. Used by permission. All rights reserved.

Scripture quotations marked (NLT) are taken from the *Holy Bible, New Living Translation*, copyright © 1996. Used by permission of Tyndale House Publishers, Inc., Wheaton, Illinois 60189. All rights reserved.

Scripture quotations marked (NKJV) are taken from the *New King James Version*®, copyright © 1982 by Thomas Nelson, Inc. Used by permission. All rights reserved.

The opinions expressed by the author are not necessarily those of Tate Publishing, LLC.

Published by Tate Publishing & Enterprises, LLC
127 E. Trade Center Terrace | Mustang, Oklahoma 73064 USA
1.888.361.9473 | www.tatepublishing.com

Tate Publishing is committed to excellence in the publishing industry. The company reflects the philosophy established by the founders, based on Psalm 68:11,
"The Lord gave the word and great was the company of those who published it."

Book design copyright © 2010 by Tate Publishing, LLC. All rights reserved.
Cover design by Lance Waldrop
Interior design by Nathan Harmony

Published in the United States of America
ISBN: 978-1-61566-138-1
Religion: Christian Life: General
10.05.11

Dedication

I dedicate this book to a very precious daughter of God, in honor of the promises of the Almighty God because I love you and I understand your disappointments, pain, tears, struggles, and your hopes, desires, and dreams. Thank you for allowing me to share a very personal and hurtful part of your life in the opening of this book.

This is also dedicated to all the young unwed mothers, abandoned wives, and single fathers left to raise their children alone without the other spouse or parent. Also to children and teens that have been abandoned or have lost both parents due to rejection, sickness, wars, or some other tragic event, to assure you God has not forsaken you and a time has been appointed to bless you through and through.

This book is written to share and remind all who encounter it that the Lord God Almighty has a plan for every life and a purpose for everything in it and that the Lord is sovereign over our lives. He has promised never to leave us or forsake us. He sees, he hears, he cares, and he does indeed answer our prayers.

I pray that God would soon remember his promise to turn the hearts of the fathers back to the children and the children to the fathers so that there be no curse on the land, according to Malachi 4:6.

I pray that all of humanity will come to know our Creator, that we all become completely intimate with him and his will for our lives, and that we all fulfill our God-Appointed Destiny (GAD)!

"GAD" was one of the twelve sons of Jacob (Israel), and one of the tribes of the children of Israel. The name Gad means, *"Destiny" "Good fortune" or "He has turned my luck."* The Lord God Almighty is a God of good fortune, the God of our destiny and a God who certainly knows how to turn your life around. Amen!

> *For I know the plans I have for you," says the* LORD. *"They are plans for good and not for disaster, to give you a future and a hope.*
>
> Jeremiah 29:11(NLT)

Acknowledgments

First and foremost, all glory and honor to God Most High, the Maker of heaven and earth and everything beneath it. I give an abundance of thanks to the triune God of my fathers, to my heavenly Father, Elohim (the Creator and sustainer of all life), who lovingly cares and watches over us with an everlasting love. To his only begotten Son, Jesus of Nazareth, who willfully chose to die for our sins that we may be reconciled back to God and that we may attain his gift of eternal life, and to the Holy Spirit who lives within the hearts of all who believe and truly know him.

I thank you, Yeshua (Jesus), the Son of God, the Messiah, who chose to die for us, providing a way for us to be reconciled with our heavenly Father. Thank you, Father, for delivering us from the power of sin and death and transporting us from out of the kingdom of darkness into the kingdom of your dear son, according to Colossians 1:13 (*KJV*). Thank you for justification, sanctification, and the gift of everlasting life.

Thank you Holy Spirit, the Spirit of Truth, our Comforter, Friend and Trusted Mentor, the one who leads and guides us to know truth and helps us all through life by filling our lives with love, wisdom, knowledge, and understanding of the true God and the purpose and meaning of life. I love you, heavenly Father, I love you, Jesus, and I love you, Holy Spirit.

To my grandmother, Mrs. Lucille Madlock, who's gone home to be with the Lord and my mother, Sarah Jenkins, who is still with us. I thank God for both of you because it was through both of you that our family was given the truth, the knowledge, and the opportunity to receive Jesus Christ. Through both of you, we saw goodness, mercy, and truth, and we experienced above all your sacrificial love. Thank you for displaying to us the love of our Lord and Savior, Jesus Christ.

Momma, thank you for giving me physical life. Thank you for your unconditional love and prayers. Thank you for setting a godly example for all of us to follow. And I thank the Lord for giving you a love and the wisdom to see and support the things that interested each of your children. You supported and nurtured our gifts and talents from childhood.

I was very moved when you told me about the persecution you endured at work, being determined to stay because of your children. It was then that I realized how great your love is for us. You laid your life down then, and you continue to do so for us today. There were times I shared with you some negative things that occurred in my childhood, and each time your first response was, "Where was I? I didn't know!" So I wrote this poem in dedication to you, Momma.

Where Was I?

Where was I? You want to know?
You were here, Momma, loving us so.

It was your words that soothed the scars in our hearts;
You knew just what to say for all our sensitive parts.

You were behind our happy smiles, during our school plays,
Because it was your face we saw in
the audience those days.

You were behind the bandages, on our elbows and knees,
From falls on our bikes, skates, and the big
swings we made on Grand-momma's trees.

Where was I? You want to know?
You were here Momma, loving us so.

You told me one day you skipped many meals,
making sure we all had plenty to eat.
We never knew, because we always had
meals, clothes, and shoes for our feet.

When you told me of how you were among
the first blacks hired at G.E.
You endured great racial persecution,
but determined to stay, having mouths to feed.

I was shocked and grieved because
I couldn't believe my ears,
As your eyes filled with tears from the
pain you endured those years.

Forgive us, Momma, for the unnecessary
trouble I'm sure we caused you;

*We were just kids, not realizing the pain and
struggles you were already going through.*

*There were many days you didn't get much rest;
Yet still for us, you continued to give your very best.*

*Where was I? You want to know?
You were here Momma, loving us so.*

*Now I understand the power of sacrifice;
It's love, dying to self; to give of one's life.*

*You couldn't have displayed the love of God any better;
You were always here for us no matter what the weather.
You laid for us a beautiful foundation,
You gave us lots of love, understanding,
and tremendous patience.*

*You are a faithful wife, and you are a marvelous mother,
before my eyes and those of my sisters and brothers.*

*You have given us a wonderful life and a legacy,
You prepared the ways for us to be blessed,
through your integrity.*

*You have shown us the way to the Lord Jesus Christ,
And you presented us the opportunity
to receive the gift of eternal life.*

*Now by the grace of God, I'm striving
to give you all that I can,
To honor and love you while I still have a chance.*

*I am determined with all the gifts and
creative ability God has given me,
To help provide for your present and your future needs.*

Momma, you are indeed worthy of praise,
Great is your reward from the Ancient of Days.

Where was I? Now you know!
You were here, Momma, loving us so.

I love you, Momma!
—Be' Trice

Words of Thanks

To my Father, Bennie L. Jenkins, who, in the midst of the publishing of this book, went home to be with the Lord on July 4, 2009. Thank you for your love, protection and your hand of correction. You provided for us and helped to keep my feet on the path of doing right. You left me many memories to cherish. I love you and miss you greatly.

To my brothers, Cory, Rickey, and Rodney Jenkins, you guys never gave me a minute's trouble. (Smile!) You all are good guys. I love you all very much. Rickey, I want to give you very special thanks. It was through you that the Lord drew me back into a right relationship with him. Your commitment to our Lord helped to put me back on the right path to my life's pre-planned destiny. Thank you for the awesome part you have played in my life. I love you very much.

To my sister, Bridgette L. Jenkins, you are the best sister and friend a girl could ever have. Your caring ways are immeasurable, and so is your integrity. You are indeed a wonderful, virtuous woman, worthy of much praise. Whenever I need you, you are always available. Thank you for being here for me. Thank you for your precious time, patience's and devotion in helping me fulfill my dreams. I will always cherish your love and sisterhood.

To my younger sister, Belander E. Hodges, who certainly understands the power of laughter. You were behind all the glamour hairstyles, and you help me to maintain my joy and big smiles. Whenever I needed a dose of laughter, I knew just who to call—my younger sister, "Tuttie." I love you.

To my sister-in-law Kashena Jenkins and your mother, Mrs. Dorothy Thomas; Thank you for your love and kindness you both show toward my family and the loving care you gave my father. May the Lord tremendously bless you both.

To my brother-in-law, Charles Hodges, I love you.

To my nephews Keith, Christopher, Charles Jr., Cody, Damiyon, Deion and to my niece Erica, I love you all.

To the late Pastor Mike Martin, who's gone home to be with the Lord and to his wife, Mrs. Beverly Martin, of Emmanuel Baptist Church. It was through your ministry that the Lord began to thoroughly develop me in his Word. You helped me to become intimate with the Word of God by encouraging me to pray and read the Word of God daily and live life according to his words. Thank you for the work you did in helping to prepare me for the work of the ministry in the kingdom of God and Christ.

To my greatest inspirers, my pastor and his wife, Dr. Sammie and Addie Holloway, Pastor Howard and Sharon Moss, Ms. Faye Lynch, Dr. Myles Munroe, Michelle McKinney Hammond, and many other ministries that have blessed me through their teaching, such as Dr. James Dobson and all the staff and guests of Focus on the Family, Family Life Today, Family Forum, Point Of View, and the late Marlin Maddux; also Crown Ministries and co-founder, the late Larry Burkett, and many others. Thank you for your ministries and labors of love. All of you have been and are significant parts of my Christian walk with the Lord Jesus. Thank you all so very much.

I would also like to give special thanks to Pastor Willie A. Sesley and Mrs. Sesley for their love and devotion to the Lord in serving the people of God and the gifts they have imparted to me during the time I sat under their leadership. To Mrs. Sesley, I want to extend my deepest gratitude and appreciation for your time and devotion in helping me with the proofreading of not only this book, but the other books that are waiting to be published. Your gift has helped me to professionally prepare for publishing and to further the call of God on my life. Thank you very much.

To Gloria Carr, thank you for your friendship and the time you gave in assisting me with editing. May the Lord continue to keep you and fulfill all he has planned for you and your family.

To the customers of Master Needles Alteration and Tailoring Shoppes, the best customers in the world! Many of you have patronized me for years. You have blessed me financially, mentally, spiritually, and emotionally. I cannot say enough of how much you have encouraged me and spoken well of my employees and I and of the services we provide. God indeed has blessed me and made my name great through you. Thank you all for your constant patronage.

To Emiterio Paras, my devoted employee, and to Barbara Vanburen, owner of Master Needles II. Thank you both for your skillful and dedicated work in assisting all our customers. Your faithful commitment has also allowed me to work more freely on my books as well. May the Lord continue to bless you both as you have blessed me!

To my friend Phyllis Hill, whom I call, "Angel Wings." Your friendship is angelic indeed. You have always been there for me, even when I felt I couldn't go to anyone else. You have been the shoulder I needed to cry on. Your kind words of love and wisdom always pointed me to the Word of God and encouraged me to keep the faith. Thanks and much love to you, Luther Hill and the rest of the family.

Ms. Debra Williams, I thank you for your temporary services in aiding me with my customers and with the care of my home. Thank you for your friendship, your service, and your prayers, which are so greatly needed and appreciated.

Tamara Vanburen, I greatly appreciate you for your time, dedication, and educational skills. May you find grace, favor, and utmost respect in the eyes of your college professors, fellow students, and colleagues, as you pursue a degree in International Business. "You Go Girl!"

I would like to give an abundance of thanks to Audra Marvin, my editor who assisted me with a spirit of excellence. Your professional and skillful service outweighed my greatest expectation. You were extremely patient, helpful, and understanding concerning all my worries and concerns as an author. You helped me to understand some of the ins and outs of the publishing industry, preparing me to move forward with what the Lord has given me. May the Lord continue to promote you and bless all your endeavors. Thank you so very, very much.

Special thanks to Lance Waldrop, my cover designer and Nathan Harmony, my layout designer. Your talents and promptness concerning the vision of my book is greatly appreciated. You both were very professional and kind as we spoke.

Also, special thanks to Janey Hays, Dave Dolphin, Rachel

Sweeden, and the entire Tate Publishing Staff for the superb service you have given me.

Last but not least, to a very wonderful, wise, compassionate, peace-loving, and patient man of God. One whom I admire and adore greatly, Mr. Stephen Roger Yarde. You are brilliant, and I indeed am honored to know you. Your profound knowledge, wisdom, and skillful ability to articulate a message or point of view concerning any issue captivates me. It was through you that my gift of book writing was birthed, as I begin to write you concerning the spiritually deep and innermost intimate thoughts and feelings of my heart. All of which you always received with a humble and understanding spirit. Your friendship is immeasurable. You have encouraged me greatly throughout the eight years I have known you. You've always spoken positive, affirming the gifts and calling the Lord has given me. Before you knew I had already begun to write the first book, you said, and I quote:

"Be' Trice! One day you are going to write a book, and in some small way, I will be a part of it!"

Today those words have manifested. Thank you for being in my life. I love you profusely.

You all have blessed me and inspired me in such a way that I would have to write another book in order to explain how. This book has come forth as a testimony and as a result of what your love, your inspiration, and your words of encouragement have done. It is also the evidence of the Lord's presence in my life, being revealed from chapter to chapter. And that our God loves us and he sees, hears, and answers our prayers. Thank you all very much, and may the Lord return to you a hundredfold of what you have poured into me. May the Lord continue to keep and prosper you all in the majestic name of the true and living God—Jesus, the Christ, our Lord. Amen.

My Mission

My mission and greatest desire, with the help of the Holy Spirit, is to take the word of God to people everywhere through the medium of books, tapes, and public speaking.

My mission is to encourage you to know our Creator God and his only begotten Son, the Lord Jesus Christ, who suffered a brutal beating unlike no man has or will ever experienced, and then died for us, by giving up his life so that through him we may receive forgiveness for our sins and be reconciled back to God.

My mission is to share with all humanity that we have been given the greatest gift of all, the gift of eternal life, which can only be received through our Creator and Redeemer of life—Jesus, the Son of God.

My mission is to present some of the most beautiful and wonderful events of human experiences concerning life, love, and Lord, revealed in God's Word and to bring joy and freedom to people of all ages by unlocking their minds and hearts with the power of the gospel of Jesus Christ.

My mission is to provoke, encourage, and motivate Non-Believers to know the Lord; and to the Believers, that they pursue a more meaningful and intimate relationship with our Creator; and to clearly define how an individual can pinpoint and fulfill his or her God-appointed destiny.

My mission is to remind us all that every one of us will stand before the God of love, mercy, and judgment to give an account for our lives and be rewarded accordingly.

> *The Spirit of the Sovereign Lord is upon me, because the Lord has appointed me to bring good news to the poor. He has sent me to comfort the brokenhearted and to announce that captives will be released and prisoners will be freed. He has sent me to tell those who mourn that the time of the Lord's favor has come, and with it, the day of God's anger against their enemies.*
>
> Isaiah 61:1–2 (NLT)

Table of Contents

23	Introduction
33	My Prayer for You
35	The Last Tear
55	The Power of A Positive Father
63	The Love & Sovereignty of the Almighty
111	Knowing Your Child's Destiny Before Birth
145	Child-Less
159	A Reason and A Season
175	Purposely Designed After Its Own Kind
203	Life, Liberty and Lucre
239	God Is In Charge
247	Redeem the Time
253	Prayer for Salvation

Introduction

Welcome! Welcome! Welcome! Your timing couldn't have been better. *"God's Appointed Destiny (GAD)"* presents *"Life, a Pre-Planned Destiny."* It is the first of five books. The other four books are simply waiting to be polished and published.

Throughout my relationship with the Lord, he has taught me many wonderful things from his Word, through the Holy Spirit. And through those who have taught me the Word of God over the years. My life is full and over flowing, and the Holy Spirit is constantly filling me with more wisdom and knowledge. Having a great desire to share the many beautiful things I have learned, I asked:

"Lord, how can I share all these wonderful truths that have been poured into me over the years?"

These are the words he loving and gently spoke to me:

"Put it in a book. It's your biggest audience. There are people who will not read the Bible, even some in the church, but they will read a book."

Mission accomplished!

You are about to embark upon a very insightful and exuberating journey that will uplift you, encourage you, refresh you, and set your life upon a path that it was predestined for. Please know that while on this journey we will need to make several detours in order to get to our desired destination because we will run into numerous obstacles, such as troubled waters, mountains, and valleys. That's life! In other words, there are always people, things, and events we encounter in life causing discouragement and distress, hindrances, and distractions to throw us off course and sometimes, throw in the towel. So it may seem I'm turning and changing the subject a bit, but these turns are just detours along the way to ensure you get a greater understanding and a bigger picture of what is being said. And as lengthy as this intro may seem, it introduces you to heart of the following books as well.

Do you struggle with knowing your purpose in life? Do you feel like God has forgotten about you? Like you've been beaten down and have reached the last of your patience? If so, take heart! *God's Appointed Destiny* will show you multiple examples from Scripture where many of God's chosen servants went through the worst of trials and even lost hope. Their faith wavered, just like ours does. Some chose not to believe God, just as many of us often do. *God's Appointed Destiny* shows that patience, purpose, passion, and prayer will get even the most doubtful of Christians through the toughest times. It shows how trials causes Non-Christians to believe and accept the truth that God is who he says he is and does what he says he will do.

Here on the pages of this appointed book, are words of profound wisdom, knowledge, and understanding both from spiritual and natural laws. These laws have been, are, and shall always be God's given laws and principles for all life. These laws and principles are for our benefit, and when we honor God and his laws, God and his laws will honor us. Throughout this entire journey, with the gracious help of the Holy Spirit, I have included, biblical truths from the King James Bible, the New King James Bible, the Amplified Bible, and of course my favorite, the New Living Translation Bible, as a witness, to declare and enforce the things I have written for you; Also, characters from biblical history, recent history, and present history as further evidence.

Men, women and young people wrestle all through life with truth, faith, religion, purpose, love, relationships, health, governments and money. Millions are frustrated and angry and some have become bitter, due to the foolishness and corruption of others and sometimes due to their own mistakes and sins. *God's Appointed Destiny* explains why this happens and how to overcome these battle cries of life. You will encounter numerous examples showing that God appoints and controls the destinies of people, nations, governments, wars, money, and even the wicked. And though we go through the worst of times, even losing hope in those darkest hours, the sovereignty of the Lord Almighty is still at work on our behalf, bringing us into our pre-planned destiny.

Here in the last few years, I too had become frustrated and grievously concerned about our generation and the one we have produced. Our nation praises and promotes infidelity, infidels, and infamous living more and more. Please don't anyone misunderstand me. I love my country, but it grieves me to see so many of the things practiced here that God said would destroy nations. Some institutions are full of corruption. Some have lost their meaning and purpose for their existence.

Corruption is all around us. There's the constant devaluation of moral values, such as the sanctity of marriage and the protection of human life. Instead of valuing these things, they value the profits from the promotions of sexual immorality, through several mediums—the internet, television, magazines, catalogs, music, fashion industry and entertainment industry! Though it is used by some to produce and promote good, it is also used by others as a weapon to cause division, deception, depression and destruction.

We have a leadership that for years has been slow to crack down on adult and child pornography. In fact, it has increased even more on the internet, at the click of a fingertip, or lying right in the palm of a hand. Pornography is one of the biggest money-making industries in the world. You will be shocked at some of the well known corporations that are making millions off this industry every year. Detailed documentation of the pornography industry and the companies involved, in what is one of the biggest billion dollar industries in the world, can be viewed at this site under the title "Porn Nation": http://www.cwfa.org/articles/2041/CWA/pornography/index.htm.

I am astonished at the free rein this industry has been given. I say this because some of these producers of pornography appeared to Wall Street for more investors and Washington for some bailout money too. Now why did they feel they had the right and the freedom to do so, if it is illegal? How can these big corporations get kick backs if it's illegal? How can they get kick backs if they don't know who they are or where to find them? Doesn't it stand to reason they know where they are, especially when so many of their colleagues and constituents have fallen prey, and some even resigned due to their involvement? Of course! So why is so little being done? "Profits"!

If you see a poor person being oppressed by the powerful and justice being miscarried throughout the land, don't be surprised! For every official is under orders from higher up, and matters of justice only get lost in red tape and bureaucracy. Even the king milks the land for his own profit!
                                                Ecclesiastes 5:8–9 (NLT)

Well, that explains why the constitutional laws concerning obscene and indecent exposure and materials, are not being regulated by the FCC (Federal Communications Commission), who is commissioned by a higher authority, the U.S. Congress.

The word of God is true and right and it has the answers to all the issues of life. Now if a government can set an eye in the sky to track the activities on the earth, they can certainly track and crack down on the corruptible things that are destroying our nation. It is an awesome blessing that the Almighty God has given man, ability to accomplish such great achievements like satellites and Google Earth, but have we forgotten; there's another eye in the sky watching our nation and all the other nations of the world.

For by his great power he rules forever. He watches every movement of the nations; let no rebel rise in defiance.
                                                Psalm 66:7 (NLT)

American is one of the world's most beautiful and happiest places to live, but it is sad and hurtful to see what is happening to her every day. We have lost our way. We have forsaken our nation's appointed purpose and destiny. America! The one appointed before she was ever founded, to be a beacon of light and righteousness to her citizens and other nations around the world. It is grievous to see the corruption, the lasciviousness and every other evil practice taking place here and around the world and I can't help but wonder how much more can the earth endure, especially here in the good ole' USA.

After observing all these things, I wondered too, how could the next generation survive from what our generation has sown and produced for them? Many have termed our youth generation as *Generation X* because of their lack of respect and regard for governmental laws, human life, and very little reverence or fear of God. Laws are being twisted and new ones added, while at the same time they are trying to muzzle the mouth and will of the God of the Christians, who created, blessed and protects this nation every day, yet they embraces and gives free rein to the teachings of other religions from other nations. We have generations of people, young and old, casting off all restraints because some in our branches of government and some in other places of authority—international and domestic—have abandoned the very things that bring restraint; the laws of the land; and the laws of the true and living God.

> *Where there is no revelation, the people cast off restraint; but happy is he who keeps the law.*
>
> Proverbs 29:18 (NKJV)

Some have described this great country of ours as "a nation without a conscience." This simply and clearly describes and classifies the nature of the generation before it because it is the one that delivered it and the ones training, molding, and shaping it. However, I think a more defining term for this young generation that we have produced would be better termed as the *Exit Generation*, marking the time and event when the righteous may exit this world. An event taught and described in the Word of God as *catching away*. This term is also described in a more modern term as *the rapture of the body of Christ*. It has been said by many spirit-filled Christian pastors and prophetic teachers that we are the generation where the Lord Jesus will come for his church, the body of Christ. Although we do not know the exact day or hour, the signs of that time the Lord warned us of are all around us and are unfolding every day. One can't help but notice the rampant increase of signal changes in the weather, such as cold temperatures in the summer season and summer temperatures in the winter season. Scientific studies show hurricanes and tornados increasing in alarming numbers, reports of tsunamis wiping out thousands, and gigantic waves of water seventy feet high slammed against the side of a cruise ship, knocking off the top-deck furniture. Even now, news reporters call it "wicked weather!" But they dare not call the ungodly behavior of mankind wicked.

Then, there are more and more wars and talks of wars, terrorism, suicide bombings, talks of nuclear wars, the increased exposure of crimes in high places, the rampant rise of infidelity, increase of promiscuous lifestyles among our youth, the promotion of adult and child pornography and its easy access right up to the palm of your hand, increase of sexual predators at any age, human trafficking, rise of deception, etc.

We live in a country where infamous living is an honorable practice; where infidelity has become the norm; where pedophiles are created; sexual immorality is promoted and praised and where our youths are encouraged to indulge in a life of promiscuity, rather than a life of productivity.

We are destroying the destiny of our nation's children. They are being robbed of their future every day. Our nation has become intoxicated with sex and love for money. Children are being used for sexual pleasures and babies' body parts are sold for profits. Legally! Things are being done to children that a dog wouldn't do. A dog by instinct will automatically protect a child, unless it has been trained to attack. Yet some adults, even some parents, will rob their own children of their innocence because of their corrupt and uncontrollable sexual appetites.

Abortion clinics snuff out the life of a baby just as their fragile little heads begins to exit the womb of its mother, under a slick little title called *partial-birth abortion* (part of the way out of the womb). The Lord said these kinds of evils, shock the heavens. All these things are taking place right under the table of our *God-Bless-America* Christian nation. Some stand and say, "God Bless America," while their actions go contrary to his word. There are other countries where a certain religious group of people will hang you or cut your throat if you speak in opposition to their religion or the gods they worship. I do not say we should do the same, but we should not give a platform to those who mock the Lord our God, his name, or his people in our own country. The Lord God Almighty is the one who loves us and has poured out his blessings upon this nation, above many other nations.

Our leaders are like parents. They are the overseers of the nation and the citizens to whom the nation belongs. They are the ones who are to see to it that those in positions of authority over the citizens carry out the duty of law already established by the owner of the land, who is the Almighty God and the house establishers, who are the founding forefathers. However, many of them have lost sight of the nation's true vision and their roles required to fulfill it.

The stork knows the time of her migration, as do the turtledove, the swallow, and the crane. They all return at the proper time each year. But not my people! They do not know what the Lord requires of them.
                                        Jeremiah 8:7 (NLT)

In the mist of these troubling times, I continued to ask the Lord for more of his wisdom and knowledge. I asked him for a deeper meaning and understanding into the ways of life. I asked him to show me more of how he views people, money, and relationships. Three things the Lord revealed to me as he guided me in prayer and through the pages of his Book of Life, the Holy Bible. This is what I understood:

People seek money, relationships, and sexual gratification; All 3 of these things mankind seeks before pursuing the gifts and callings that I have given to them.

Life is not a haphazard experience, but rather, it is about a Loving God who created us for his glory. He wants us to know him and the things concerning his son Jesus, the things he has preplanned for our life, our service to our generation and to those after us. Every generation needs the same gifts and calling for service in order for it to function, sustain, and properly grow. We all have gifts that people and the world need.

The Holy Spirit went on to help me to understand a more in-depth picture as to why millions of lives are lost and totally out of order. Millions of people do not know anything about themselves or their purpose in life, and then they go to pursue a relationship with someone who doesn't know who they are either. Then these same persons combine their lack of knowledge in this, and they come together in sexual union and bring more children on the earth to pattern after them. Therefore, this lack of knowing who you are and your purpose is passed down on and on and on for generations; People wandering upon the earth not being fulfilled or bringing fulfillment to the lives of others. And worse than that is to not know the Lord, our Creator.

Millions fail to see that God has an agenda too—one that is higher and far greater than ours. However, he does not keep everything a secret. He reveals his mind and plan to those who want to know it. It's laid out in his Word and revealed to us by his Spirit as we spend time with him.

The Lord loves us, and he wants what is best for us and has shown us how to get the best out of life now and forever in the Bible. Nevertheless, people still come and go, even Christians, never having known their purpose or gifts and callings. There is a myth that says, "*What you don't know can't hurt you,*" but the truth of the matter is, what you don't know can destroy you! And one of the wisest and greatest teachers of the Word of God, Dr. Myles Munroe, said, "The graveyards are full of unfulfilled potential." This doesn't have to be our legacy, nor our children.

God's Appointed Destiny will help you pinpoint your gifts and calling and those of your children, even before their birth. Once recognized, you can better prepare for your life's preplanned destiny. You will see and understand that God is sovereign over us, and even in our darkest hours, he is still working out his will for us. The Lord is concerned about every part of our lives. He is the one who controls our destiny, because he is the one who called it to be. And he wants to fulfill it in and through both you and me.

My Prayer for You

Heavenly Father, thank you for the marvelous opportunity you have given me to share your words of life and peace. And thank you for blessing the works of my hands. According to your word, if Jesus be lifted up, you will draw all people to yourself. Use this book to draw every near and distant heart closer to you. Holy Spirit, open the eyes of every reader's understanding so that they will be able to comprehend the deep and beautiful truths of this book. Fill every heart with the glorious light of God's rich word. Cause every reader to understand the wonderful future you have promised to all who accept your beloved son Jesus and your calling for their lives. Help them to clearly understand the rich and glorious inheritance you have pre-planned for each of us, before, the world, begun. Refresh every heart, restore every soul, and heal every hurt. Help each reader to diligently and willingly accept and live in accordance to your statutes and commandments, where all of life's treasures and true happiness is found. In the majestic name of our Lord and Savior, Jesus, The True and Living Christ and King, Amen!

The Last Tear

Not one tear falls from our eyes and our Heavenly Father not see it!

You keep track of all my sorrows.
You have collected all my tears in your bottle.
You have recorded each one of them in your book.
Psalm 56:8 (NLT)

Tears of pain mixed with anger and frustration rolled down her lovely, dark brown cheeks. She said she could not understand why she and her siblings had to endure the things that grieved them so about their father. Turning slightly away, not wanting me to see her tears as she wiped them from her face, she spoke of the things that angered and hurt them so much.

"We hate to be at home sometimes. We're always asking Momma if we can go with her." She expressed with great anguish how she was accused of not being any good because she had become pregnant at fifteen years of age.

As I sat listening to this young girl's story, I thought of how so many of us ourselves or someone we know can relate to her story and pain. This same father had several children out of wedlock. He smokes, drinks, and does drugs regularly and let a twenty-year-old feller get away with impregnating his fifteen-year-old daughter. Yet he tells her she isn't any good and will never amount to anything.

She said she was accused of being the cause for their family falling apart. As she spoke, I thought to myself how her father is totally oblivious to the fact that he is a major cause of their family falling apart and an indirect cause of her pregnancy.

She stated several times that he insisted she have an abortion and was adamant that her mother should be the one to take her. In other words, he was saying, *Honey, take our daughter and have our grandchild put away.*

This is how dark and evil the human heart can be without the presence and fear of God in it. Yet no matter how dark the heart, God will change it when we sincerely ask.

> *The human heart is most deceitful and desperately wicked. Who really knows how bad it is? But I know! I, the Lord, search all hearts and examine secret motives. I give all people their due rewards, according to what their actions deserve.*
>
> Jeremiah 17:9–10 (NLT)

> *Create in me a clean heart, O God. Renew a right spirit within me.*
>
> Psalm 51:10 (NLT)

Millions of innocent little lives have been snuffed out because people don't realize (and some refuse to accept the truth) that human life begins at conception. They argue, "Well it's our body and we can choose to do with it whatever we want."

Though this might be true for you, the small innocent little body forming inside the womb belongs to another. The baby!

Some say, "Well, what if the mother was raped or her health was at risk? Shouldn't she have a right to choose?" Definitely! And if she is told and understands the whole truth, she would want that child to live. As for her health being at risk, it greatly depends on the circumstances, but most mothers are more likely to choose life for their children over their own lives.

> *Today I have given you the choice between life and death, between blessings and curses. I call on heaven and earth to witness the choice you make. Oh, that you would choose life, that you and your descendants might live!*
> Deuteronomy 30:19 (NLT)

This father isn't alone in this though. This mentality has become an epidemic among the male nation. Many men and women too are so lost and caught up in their own sinful and selfish indulgence that they cannot see themselves and the hurt they are causing their own children. Like so many others, he was not willing to accept the fact that the drugs and alcohol he had been indulging in for years were a major cause of his family's troubles, not only in *their* lives, but also his very own.

Now, what about the twenty-year-old feller who got his daughter pregnant? What did he do about him? Nothing! According to our law, that is statutory rape. She was only fifteen! When a grown man uses you and the other accuses you, what can a young girl do? Whom do our daughters look to for love, protection, help, and guidance? Her mother, another woman; another young girl; or perhaps another man like her father!

When you look around the land it looks like the fathers and husbands are slowly vanishing from the earth. I didn't say they had, but it sure looks like, especially among the African American community. One thing is for sure, women often out live the men.

Some of you may be thinking and saying, *Well, this is the world we live in!* No, I disagree. This is not the world we have to live in, but it is the world men and women have created for our children and the next generations to live in, and it does not have to be this way. We created it through our behaviors and demonstrating to them how they are to live and think. When men and women rebel against the laws of God and the land, their children are prone to follow. Train a generation right, right they shall go! Train a generation wrong, wrong they shall go! Either way, they are trained by the generation before them. And God commanded parents to train children in the way they should go, especially the fathers.

> *Train up a child in the way he should go: and when he is old, he will not depart from it.*
> Proverbs 22:6 (KJV)

> *And now a word to you fathers. Don't make your children angry by the way you treat them. Rather, bring them up with the discipline and instruction approved by the Lord.*
> Ephesians 6:4 (NLT)

Many times, we are unable to see ourselves as well as others, so it's always good to ask the Lord to show us ourselves, or a friend, even a family member—someone we know will be honest with us. It's not always a pretty picture, but we need to do so in order that we may recognize where we are and what we need to do to bring about positive changes or improvements.

Here are three of the best ways to see what we really look like: 1) Look at the leaders of our nation and others in authority. 2) Look at the youth generation, and 3) Look at the Word of God. Now compare each group to the word of God and see how we mirror it. If anybody's home should reflect the word of God, it's the people of God. If not, let's get with the program laid out in his word, so our families and nation can continue to receive the blessings and not the cruses spoken of in his word.

> *Discipline your children, and they will give you happiness and peace of mind. When people do not accept divine guidance, they run wild. But whoever obeys the law is happy.*
> Proverbs 29:17–18 (NLT)

What overwhelming pressure this mother and daughter must have been under. They both were totally against the abortion. Her mother was advised that she should not be the one to live with that guilt. If he insisted, then let him be the one to do it, but under no circumstance should she go against her convictions, or violate the Word of God. Thank God, this baby's life was spared. She was able to bring forth a healthy and happy baby boy.

It's troublesome to think that one day that little fellow and other children, who escaped the hands of the abortionist, will grow up and look into the eyes of those who once thought or attempted to cut off their life. Sometimes we really don't realize just how dark and evil the human heart is. But to know and fear the Lord is to hate evil. I know that today this grandfather is very happy they didn't go through with it.

Sometimes we can think and do the worst things when we are under pressure, but when we calm down and give ourselves proper time to reason things out, we often make the right decision. Life is precious to the Lord, and so is the death of his people, even an unborn infant. The average mind would think why would God be grieved? Don't they go to be with him? Yes, the innocent children and those who have received his plan of salvation through Jesus Christ. I believe the reason death grieves the Lord, is because from the beginning when he created Adam and Eve, he had always intended for us to live and never die. God loves life, not death. At the great white throne judgment, death is thrown in the lake of fire.

> *The LORD's loved ones are precious to him; it grieves him when they die.*
> Psalm 116:15 (NLT)

> *The sea gave up the dead who were in it, and Death and Hades delivered up the dead who were in them. And they were judged, each one according to his works. Then Death and Hades were cast into the lake of fire. This is the second death. And anyone not found written in the Book of Life was cast into the lake of fire.*
> Revelation 20:13–15 (NKJV)

When she was accused of being the cause of their family's trouble, her older brother, who was eighteen at the time, heard what was being said from another room in the house. He came to her aid by standing in the gap for her against those false accusations. Her brother told their father that he didn't have to continue badgering her, tearing her down, and telling her she was no good and would never be anything, but instead he should be affirming her. He told him, "*We all make mistakes and she will be okay and can still make something of herself.*"

He was certainly right. We all do. In fact, many of our mistakes are called sin, and sometimes we repeat them over and over until will finally get it right. I dare not say this young girl was not partially responsible for her becoming pregnant. She certainly was to a certain degree. But as I said before and will say it again, when parents rebel against the Lord and his way of life, the children are prone to follow.

When men fell to stand in the gap for their children, the Lord still has a ram in the bush. He used a teenage son. Now that I think about it, he was the man God was looking for at that time. Age or physical stature does not make one a man, but the courage to stand up and do what is right is what makes a man. Never underestimate your teens! They have more courage than many of us think.

> *So I sought for a man among them who would make a wall, and stand in the gap before Me on behalf of the land, that I should not destroy it; but I found no one.*
> Ezekiel 22:30 (NKJV)

The Lord has ordained the father of the house to stand in the gap for his family, not his son, even if the father is not there. The perfect order of God is for the fathers to teach the sons what it means to be a man. He is to show them by examples what is morally right and how to be a good husband and a good father. When a man does this for his sons and daughters, he commands the blessing of God on his life and his family forever. Then and only then!

> *The Lord heard your request and said to me, "I have heard what the people have said to you, and they are right. Oh, that they would always have hearts like this, that they might fear me and obey all my commands! If they did, they and their descendants would prosper forever."*
> Deuteronomy 5:28–29 (NLT)

She went further to say that she and her brother had become very close and that he did special little things for her. He also told her of the things he plans to do for her in the future. What an amazing difference. Her brother's protection and provision caused her to draw closer to him, loving him more, but her father's behavior drove her further away. Love always draws, and it covers our sins or mistakes, while hate and strife drive you away. She said as soon as she could get a job, she was moving out.

> *Hatred stirs up strife: but love covers all sins.*
> *Proverbs 10:12 (NKJV)*

> *The LORD hath appeared of old unto me, saying, Yea, I have loved thee with an everlasting love: therefore with lovingkindness have I drawn thee.*
> *Jeremiah 31:3 (KJV)*

This same brother, one Sunday night while sitting in the service, was sitting beside me. He looked up at me during the preaching and said, "*I want to give my life to Jesus.*" I was surprised at his words because he was only eight years old. I didn't know if he really understood what he was asking.

As the pastor continued preaching, I shared with him the plan of salvation and what it meant, not sure whether he understood. He said, "*I understand, I believe, and I want Jesus.*" So at the end of the service, he and I walked to the altar, and he gave his life to the Lord Jesus. I was thinking at first, *Maybe I should wait and ask his mother*, but I hesitated not, when the Holy Spirit reminded me these words.

> *But when Jesus saw what was happening, he was very displeased with his disciples. He said to them, "Let the*

children come to me. Don't stop them! For the Kingdom of God belongs to such as these."
                                                    Mark 10:14 (NLT)

As for his mom, she was elated.

It was evidently clear that this father was lacking in giving his daughter the love and attention she really needed and deserved. A father's love and attention is a necessity that every child needs, especially his little daughters. We learn best from our fathers what men and boys are like and how they should treat us.

When love and attention are lacking in a child's life, he or she will always turn to someone or something else in search of it in order to fill that void. A need to be loved and affirmed is a hunger and desire in every human heart. When this desire has gone unfulfilled, abuse is inevitable. Many times young girls, not knowing what real love looks like, are deceived into giving their sexuality to some boy or man because they think they will fill that void. Little do they know, they are only there to fill, their own lustful sexual appetite. Many of these men and young boys, having never been taught what real love is or how to honor and respect women and girls, use them, impregnate them, and then leave them to raise their children all alone in impoverished conditions. This also leaves many of these young girls and women emotionally damaged with feelings of rejection and full of anger and resentment. And many times the children of these parents especially the sons, grow up and do the same things to their children. Very few of them every purposely stay with the mother or take on the role of being a good father to them the best they know how. Those who do are rare and precious gems.

Sadly enough, this cycle goes on and on, perpetually, from generation to generation. Many of them contract sexually transmitted diseases that lead to the termination of a pregnancy, a dream, and even their very way of life. For some women, these diseases have robbed them of the hope of ever having their first child. No matter what kind of sin is committed or when, or how, it always leads to some form of death.

> *For the wages of sin is death, but the free gift of God is eternal life through Christ Jesus our Lord.*
> Romans 6:23 (NLT)

I listened to a heartbreaking story on Focus on the Family Christian radio broadcast. A guest shared how a young teenager had attended a wide party and lost control and end up having sex. She contracted a sexually transmitted disease that caused her, to have her uterus completely removed. She was only fifteen. This promiscuous act robbed her of her ability to have children from her own womb and possibly a future husband. I have heard many sad stories like this, but those who turned to the Lord he turns their pain and sorrow into a joyful and happy end. God is good.

She went on to tell me about how their father would cuss them at times. In his attempt to discipline one of his sons who was now big enough to stand up for himself, was provoked to extreme anger and retaliated. I know of another father who cussed his children, but when he committed his life totally to the Lord, he got a brand new heart and brand new mouth. Every time you speak with him the word of God rolls off his lips. And he has a heart for souls. He wins them to the Lord every chance he gets.

Fathers, do not irritate and provoke your children to anger (do not exasperate them to resentment), but rear them (tenderly) in the training and discipline and counsel and admonition of the Lord.
Ephesians 6:4 (AMP)

And I will give you a new heart with new and right desires, and I will put a new spirit in you. I will take out your stony heart of sin and give you a new, obedient heart. And I will put my Spirit in you so you will obey my laws and do whatever I command.
Ezekiel 36:26–27 (NLT)

Complaining all the more, she was very sad and hurt, mentioning that Christmas 2003 was the worst they had ever had. "He was going to give us some money to buy some shoes for Christmas, but when I asked for the money, he said he didn't have it! He always does that," she cried. Naturally, she was upset and stated that she would never let a man do those things to her son. I looked at her baby son as he laid so innocently beside her right thigh. Then she spoke again, saying, "I'm going to take the money I make today and buy my son some shoes."

I asked her why not let his father buy them.

She said, "I can't wait around for him. He's not going to do nothing for him."

Little did she realize that she was already trapped in the syndrome of deadbeat dads. Her son too has a father who was doing to their son just what she vowed would not be. He was not loving and providing for their son's spiritual, physical, mental, emotional and financial needs.

I tried to encourage her by telling her we have to be thankful to God, not *for* all things, but *in* all things. We need to thank him for the blessings he has blessed us with all year. And I told her that Christmas is a time set aside to celebrate the birth of Jesus Christ, God's loving favor, peace, and joy. It seemed so awkward to say all this to her because all these things she and her siblings were experiencing were the total opposite of what God had given. How do you convince a young heart and mind that God wants us to be thankful for his blessings of love, peace, and goodwill when mostly they see strife, anger, abuse, and destructive behavior?

We have to be careful when we share the truth about God because we can make God look bad in the eyes of our children and others. If we fail to represent the Lord properly, it could cause people to reject him. For example, there are some women and children being physically, mentally, and emotionally abused by husbands, fathers, and even outside relatives. Please don't misunderstand me. This father was not physically beating his family. Some women believe, based on what they have been taught that they should stick it out and endure the relationships until God changes the spouse. In some circumstances, this is true, but not in the case of harmful abuses. God doesn't want anyone beaten and abused under any circumstances. Man is made in the image God, and when man does things that are contrary to the nature of God, it distorts the image and love of God.

I tried comforting her, letting her know that her mother was trying to do what she believed was right for everyone and that we were praying that God would change his heart. And that he would be the loving father God has always wanted him to be and for them to have.

Her reply was, "Well, God hasn't changed him, so why doesn't Momma do something about it?"

I told her we have to give God time, just as he has many

times given us, and to allow him to teach us and to strengthen us through the bad times as well as the good times. Yet it all seemed so helpless no matter what I said.

Constantly wiping her tears away as they fell from her beautiful, dark brown eyes, she said, "You all just don't understand."

But little did she know, I did understand, and so does the Lord. He is touched by our sorrows and our tears. I understood quite well because I could relate to the pain and rejection she was feeling, which I experienced in childhood. They are things I've carried with me all my life. The only difference was I felt I was in it alone, apart from my sisters and brothers because of my father's partiality, especially concerning my sisters and me.

Although my father did not make it a practice of cussing at his children as some fathers and mothers do, he said some things that really hurt me deep down inside. I remember one day I had done something that upset him and he said to me, "No one's going to want you because you are too fat." I have cried from time to time when I think or talk of those days. Not because I still hold them against my father, but because he is my father and things like that really hurts and they become a part of your life's memories forever.

Whoever said, "*Sticks and stones may break my bones, but words will never hurt me*" was lying! Words can cut like a knife. They can crush the human spirit or give life to it. In fact, words are spirit, and they pierce the soul, cut right through your bones, and can tear your heart apart. The words you or another person speaks not only affect *your* life, but other lives as well.

> *Gentle words bring life and health; a deceitful tongue crushes the spirit.*
> Proverbs 15:4 (NLT)

> *Those who love to talk will experience the consequences, for the tongue can kill or nourish life.*
> Proverbs 18:21 (NLT)

Harmful or negative words can cause people to have low self-esteem. They can hold you back in life from pursuing your dreams, from having a positive and loving relationship with others, evening a loving relationship with our heavenly Father God, if we allow them to! For me, the effects were more along the line of low self-esteem. Our hearts, souls, and bodies are chambers that house the memories of life, whether good or bad. And the things in our heart will effect everything we do.

> *Keep your heart with all diligence, for out of it spring the issues of life.*
> Proverbs 4:23 (NKJV)

Yes, we are scarred in spirit, soul, and body. Please know, I'm not saying these things to condemn my father, nor do I hold these things against him. I remember some fun times with him as well. But you never forget those things that hurt your heart.

My father, on the other hand, probably doesn't even remember these things, and it would be wrong for me to hold them against him. How could I? I certainly wasn't perfect. When I was a young child, I took some money that didn't belong to me. Several times I did this. Not much, but enough to buy myself some cookies and candy at the store. For some reason, I loved eating cookies. I love them so much that my sisters and brothers started calling me Cookie Monster, like the one on *Sesame Street*. But thank God, my father loved me enough to tear my tail up when I did wrong. It was his hand of correction that kept me back from one day growing up to become a thief.

My father's mother died when he was three, so I guess he had no memory of her. His relatives would always tell him whenever they saw me that I was "the spitting image" of his mother. They would even tell me to pull my pant legs up, and then they would say, "Yes, she's just like your mother. She even has legs like her." Yet I never seemed to gain his favor like my sisters did. Maybe I was a constant reminder to him subconsciously of the love and emotional bonding he never received from his mother.

Though my father accepted the Lord and provided and protected us, it was my mother who took us to church and prayed for us. She laid the foundation we needed in order to get to the place where we could know and understand the love of God and his Son, Jesus, and ask him to come into our heart. Now that the Lord lives in me, I can't give enough. I have said to the Lord many times that I don't have enough money because I have so much more giving to do. You see, the devil, who is the thief, wanted me to become a thief and destroy my life, but the Lord had pre-planned for me to be an abundant giver.

> *The thief cometh not, but for to steal, and to kill, and to destroy: I am come that they might have life, and that they might have it more abundantly.*
> John 10:10 (KJV)

My father was good in disciplining us, but he made me do certain chores around the house that he never made my sisters do, not even my brothers. Though he offend brought us things, I can remember the many times when I was left out when it came to my sisters and I. My older sister was his favorite, and my younger sister was his baby girl. I, of course, was the middle child, and as the old and truthful saying goes, *The middle child always gets it!*

He would say, "Well she gets it because she is the oldest, or she gets it because she is the youngest." Being a child this never sat well with me, and I became somewhat distant in my love for him, unlike my sisters. For years I couldn't understand why, nor could I describe the feelings I experienced.

I have learned that many times when we hurt, we fill that void with things like shopping or food or some people lose themselves into their work, some indulge in unlawful sex, even drugs, in order to bring comfort to those areas in our lives that are hurting and void of love and life. I guess that is why I loved cookies so much. They were my sweetness. Today, I still love cookies, but I try not to eat them as much.

Although wounds in time heal, the scars remain still. They become a part of your life forever. Life is full of pain and disappointments. They are what many call *lemons*. And I have learned that the lemons of life are for making lemonade, and the Lord is the sweetener.

> *But You, O Lord, are a shield for me, my glory and the One who lifts up my head.*
>
> Psalms 3:3 (NKJV)

> *How sweet are your words to my taste, sweeter than honey to my mouth!*
>
> Psalms 119:103 (NKJV)

In the midst of the editing stage of this book, my Daddy became very sick around 1 a.m. Wednesday morning, June 24, 2009. My youngest brother Rodney, who was his caregiver, went to my Daddy's room to check on him in the night. He found Daddy breathing very hard, and he wasn't able to wake him up. The ambulance immediately rushed him to the hospital. The doctors said he had another stroke, bigger than the first one, which was on last Easter Sunday of 2008. He was very weak and fragile, and they didn't think he would get any better. In fact, they suggested we put him in Hospice Care, but everyone was still hoping and praying for his recovery.

On Sunday morning, June 28, 2009, as we were sitting around his hospital bed, my younger sister Belander shared with us a dream she'd had that morning. We all laughed as she was telling it, because it was fun, crazy and yet its implication was beautiful at the same time. My Mother and I said the dream may have a meaning. So we begin to meditate on her dream more and more as she shared it. Then I said to them, "I think the Lord is letting us know Daddy is not going to make it. He is going over to the other side of life, and it will be in seven days."

On Saturday, July 4, 2009, around nine a.m., as I was leaving the hospital for work, my brother Rickey arrived so my father would never be alone. Just as I arrived at my office building, I walked in the door and my sister's dream came to mind. As I thought of it, it grieved me and I said aloud to myself, "Seven days." Then I went in, put my keys down, turned on the light and began pulling out my orders for the day. Just minutes later my mother called and said we need to go back to the hospital.

When I walked into Daddy's hospital room, my brother was staring out the window. I looked at Daddy and his head was slightly tilted to his right as if asleep and I said, "He's gone, Rickey?"

He said, "Yes! And it was so amazing. I didn't even hear him when he passed."

It was exactly seven days from the day of my sister's dream that Daddy went home to be with the Lord. Because it was

Independence Day, I said to my brother, "There are no limitations on him now."

Then my brother said, "Yes! He is free indeed!"

When the rest of the family arrived, the hospital requested information concerning his remains. As we began making preparations for his funeral, I began to reflect back on the days with him. I remembered some sweet moments with him, and then I began to remember how his hand of correction was harder on me than my other siblings. The devil always tempts us to focus on the negative things, but the Holy Spirit began to encourage my heart, by reminding me of this verse.

> *For the Lord corrects those he loves, just as a father corrects a child in whom he delights.*
> Proverbs 3:12 (NLT)

When I was young I did not understand why. But as I began to grow in the word of God, I came to know this. And I am glad my father was good at disciplining me when I needed it, and for that I can say, I am truly thankful. I know he did all he knew how to do.

I notice too, that there seem to be a connection concerning my Daddy and the Holidays. He loved celebrating the holidays with us. He always brought bags of candy to give out on Halloween night. He decorated the house for us every Christmas and he celebrated the New Year. Of all the major holidays, I believe July 4th was his favorite, because every year no matter how hot it was, he would stand over the grill and bar-b-que for us all day long. I can see him now, throwing a white towel he used to wipe his sweat, over his shoulders. Among this, the Social Security Office has him on record as being born January 1st, but my Daddy said he was born January 3rd. Funny! I am inclined to believe them, because of how he celebrated the holidays. And I can see no better day than for him to step into eternity, than on July 4th.

In honor of my father, I was chosen to be on program to do the reflections for his funeral. I shared Proverbs 3:12 with them and then I teased my sisters and brothers, saying to them, "Now I understand why his hand of correction was the heaviest on me. It was because he delighted in me the most." Then I said to them, "Take that, you siblings!" Oh boy! Did that get a big laugh!

The Holy Spirit also encouraged my heart as he reminded me of other things concerning my daddy. But in my heart I felt the Holy Spirit comforting me, saying to me, *like you, his sins are forgiven.* Then the Holy Spirit spoke this to my heart saying: *Three things your father did that he will be greatly rewarded for. He never abandoned his children, he never divorced his wife so he could marry another, and he gave me the one thing I want most from a marriage union. Godly children!*

> *Didn't the Lord make you one with your wife? In body and spirit you are his. And what does he want? Godly children from your union. So guard yourself; remain loyal to the wife of your youth.*
>
> Malachi 2:15 (NLT)

Though old tears have fallen, now new tears flow, because Daddy is greatly missed. Nevertheless, a more beautiful day is coming when we will see him again. Life indeed has its Up's and Down's, and its Win's and Loss.' But no matter what sorrows or pain we have to endure in life, a day has been appointed when the Lord himself will wipe away all tears from our eyes.

So hold your head up and smile big and wide, looking forward to that day, when God wipes away the last tear.

> *And God will wipe away every tear from their eyes; there shall be no more death, nor sorrow, nor crying. There shall be no more pain, for the former things have passed away.*
> Revelation 21:4 (NKJV)

The Power of a Positive Father

You made all the delicate inner parts of my body and knit me together in my mother's womb. Thank you for making me so wonderfully complex! Your workmanship is marvelous—and how well I know it. You watch me as I was being formed in utter seclusion, as I was woven together in the dark of the womb. You saw me before I was born. Every day of my life was recorded in your book. Every moment was laid out before a single day had passed.
Psalm 139:13–16 (NLT)

I purchased a video titled *Raising Tennis Aces (The Williams Story)*. I had no idea what I was about to see. It was astonishing! The video was an interview of Venus and Serena Williams and their father. I highly recommend that everyone get this video and listen to the words of this father concerning the destiny of these two daughters before they were conceived in their mother's womb.

In the interview, he stated that after having watched a few tennis matches on TV one evening, that he went to his wife and told her they were going to have two more children and they were going to be girls. He told her they were going to raise them to be tennis champions, and today his words are alive and well. Their next two children were girls, just like he'd said. They could have been two boys or a boy and girl, but it was two more girls. That is the power of a spoken word coming out of a believing heart.

From childhood, their father trained and shaped them into tennis aces and groomed them for success. These two sisters made it to the top and had to compete with each other for the championship. They both carry titles in Wimbledon Women's Championship Tennis.

Venus became a professional athlete at fourteen. She rose to the top, winning numerous championships and Olympic gold medals. She competed with Serena in the 2001 U.S. Open. This was the first time in all of history two sisters had made it to the final Grand Slam Tournament. In February of 2002, Venus was the first African American woman to rank #1 on the WTA Tour. Venus later started her own interior design business and her own line of clothing.

Serena, the youngest, by the age of twenty-seven, held three of the Grand Slam titles. The WTA Tour in 2002 named her player of the year, Associated Press voted Serena the best female athlete in the world, and she was named 2002 ITF Women's Singles World Champion. In 2003, Serena completed her set of Grand Slam titles, beating Venus in Melbourne, Australia. Serena has won six of the eight major finals she faced with her sister.

She also pursued a career in the fashion industry and cosmetic and contract deals with corporations like Nike. Serena has even preformed in music videos, commercials, and wrote a book with her sister titled "Serving from the Hip (Ten rules for Living, Loving, and Winning)."

On July 4, 2009, Venus and Serena once again played in a match against each other in the Wimbledon Singles, with Serena being the victor. Serena gained position as #2 World tennis player and her sister Venus fell to #3. The sisters are exceptional achievers, having numerous other accolades.

They both loved and admired their father and respected his leadership role over them. Their father walked in authority concerning their lives and made sure they were *A* students. He took careful guardianship concerning them in the media. He was very protective of them concerning their relationships with the opposite sex.

Their lives were certainly no coincidence. It was pre-planned. I'm sure there were times when raising them that their father grew weary, but the dream in his heart for them drove him on. Through racial oppression and persecution from his youth, he continued to stand his ground against those who opposed him and them.

> *What do you mean, 'If I can'? Jesus asked. Anything is possible if a person believes. The father instantly replied, I do believe, but help me not to doubt!*
> Mark 9:23 (NLT)

> *Children are a gift from the Lord; they are a reward from him.*
> Psalm 127:3 (NLT)

You know what I believe here? I believe the moment this father got a glimpse of the future concerning his next two children and declared it to his wife, the Lord looked around at his angels surrounding his throne and said to them, *Hey! Did you hear what I just heard? I like this man. I tell you I have not seen so greater faith in all of America. And I can use him and his words to proclaim and confirm my truth of what I will do for those who perceive, believe, confess, and proceed. Therefore, give this man the fruit of his lips and of the works of his hands.* And so it was.

> *People can get many good things by the words they say; the work of their hands also gives them many benefits.*
> Proverbs 12:14 (NLT)

I noticed also in this video that he didn't mention he had a relationship with the Lord. Yet he had great faith. He had the faith of the centurion soldier. The centurion soldier was a Gentile, outside of the promise covenant of Israel. Yet he believed Jesus had authority over sickness and that Jesus could heal his servant. He went to Jesus and asked him if he would just speak the word, his servant would be healed. Jesus was amazed at his faith and told him because of his faith he was going to sit in the kingdom of God along with Abraham, Isaac, and Jacob. And the Lord spoke the word, and his servant was healed in that same hour.

> *Now when Jesus had entered Capernaum, a centurion came to Him, pleading with Him, saying, "Lord, my servant is lying at home paralyzed, dreadfully tormented." And Jesus said to him, "I will come and heal him." The centurion answered and said, "Lord, I am not worthy that You should come under my roof. But only speak a word, and my servant will be healed. For I also am a man under authority, having soldiers under me. And I say to this one, 'Go,' and he goes; and to another, 'Come,' and he comes; and to my servant, 'Do this,' and he does it." When Jesus heard*

> *it, He marveled, and said to those who followed, "Assuredly, I say to you, I have not found such great faith, not even in Israel! And I say to you that many will come from east and west, and sit down with Abraham, Isaac, and Jacob in the kingdom of heaven. But the sons of the kingdom will be cast out into outer darkness. There will be weeping and gnashing of teeth." Then Jesus said to the centurion, "Go your way; and as you have believed, so let it be done for you." And his servant was healed that same hour.*
>
> Matthew 8:5–13 (NKJV)

This centurion solider was a Gentile, yet God moved for him because of his faith. As a result, he believed in Jesus, and now it has been appointed unto him a seat among the elites in the kingdom of God. How do we know this? This centurion and other fellow soldiers believed and confessed that Jesus was truly the Son of God when they saw him being crucified.

> *And Jesus cried out again with a loud voice, and yielded up His spirit. Then, behold, the veil of the temple was torn in two from top to bottom; and the earth quaked, and the rocks were split, and the graves were opened; and many bodies of the saints who had fallen asleep were raised; and coming out of the graves after His resurrection, they went into the holy city and appeared to many. So when the centurion and those with him, who were guarding Jesus, saw the earthquake and the things that had happened, they feared greatly, saying, "Truly this was the Son of God!"*
>
> Matthew 27:50–54 (NKJV)

I could be wrong, but I believe this was the same centurion who came to Jesus and asked him to heal his servant who was paralyzed. I realized that Jesus was not amazed just because the centurion had faith. He was amazed because the centurion had more faith in him than those in the covenant of Abraham—just like so many in the body of Christ today.

Many of the Gentiles among us, especially those in the business world, soar much further than many in the body of Christ while many in the body of Christ sit back and wait to go to that heavenly home in the sky. As Paul so eloquently put it, "Men and brethren this ought not to be so." We, the body of Christ, should be on top in life while accomplishing great things for the cause of Christ. Thank God we're going someday, but in the meantime Jesus said work and to take care of business until he comes. Besides, when all the days of the great tribulation are over, we are all coming back here to dwell on the new earth, under a new heaven and a new and righteous government that will never end.

> *For a child is born to us, a son is given to us. And the government will rest on his shoulders. These will be his royal titles: Wonderful Counselor, Mighty God, Everlasting Father, Prince of Peace. His ever expanding, peaceful government will never end. He will rule forever with fairness and justice from the throne of his ancestor David. The passionate commitment of the Lord Almighty will guarantee this!*
>
> Isaiah 9:6–7 (NLT)

Those in the world of business believe in going for all the gusto they can get, and I am not talking about beer. They believe in being all they can be and are not afraid to fail from trying. If one thing didn't work, they tried something else. In fact, many of them are in the business of solving problems by fixing what is broken, eliminating what needs eradicated, and updating the things that needs updating.

If God honored the faith of the centurion soldier, the Gentiles today, and the Williams sisters' father, how much more will he do for us who are called by his name? We are members of the household of God and are the heirs of his promise. "Oh ye of little faith!" Turn up the notches as high as they will go! We've much work to do. This includes me as well as the rest of you who are the true people of God and heirs of Abraham.

> *So now you Gentiles are no longer strangers and foreigners. You are citizens along with all of God's holy people. You are members of God's family.*
> Ephesians 2:19 (NLT)

The media did everything it could to discredit the Williams sisters' father, but he was not moved. He used every stone they threw at him and made stepping stones. They talked about his appearance at his daughters' tennis event and ran down everything he was doing. Yet here he was with two daughters playing for the championship title, and they've won.

I wonder where the kids of the media commentators were. What were they doing with them? What had they achieved? God didn't have a problem with the way this father was dressed, but he does have a problem with those who wrongfully judge and condemn others.

This father was a self-learner. He taught himself many things and then taught his daughters all he had learned about tennis and groomed them for public life. He was on a mission, and he wasn't going to let anything stop him. He believed in it, declared it, and put his hands to it, and God honored it. The Lord had to because this father had activated a law in the earth—the law of faith! A spoken word coming from a believing heart and the law of sowing and reaping! He and those girls sowed long, hard hours for years into their career, and they are reaping a harvest of wealth and success in return.

> *What is faith? It is the confident assurance that what we hope for is going to happen. It is the evidence of things we cannot yet see.*
> Hebrews 11:1 (NLT)

My hope and prayer for the entire Williams family, is that they come to know the Lord Jesus Christ in the pardon of their sins, because to gain the whole world and lose your soul, no manner of success can save you then.

> *For what will it profit a man if he gains the whole world, and loses his own soul? Or what will a man give in exchange for his soul?*
> Mark 8:36–37 (NKJV)

The Love & Sovereignty of the Almighty

> *When the Lord saw her, his heart overflowed with compassion. "Don't cry!" he said. Then he walked over to the coffin and touched it, and the bearers stopped. "Young man," he said, "get up." Then the dead boy sat up and began to talk to those around him! And Jesus gave him back to his mother.*
> Luke 7:13–15 (NLT)

From the beginning of creation, the Lord has seen and responded to our tears of pain and sorrow. And there is nothing like the tears of a woman or a child. Much like the beautiful young girl I spoke of in chapter one, I could see the hurt, the anger, the fear, and resentment of another young woman name Hagar. This beautiful dark skin Egyptian female slave was believed to have been taken from the land of Pharaoh and all of those she knew and loved, to the dusty tents of Abraham.

He gave Abraham gifts, for offending God when he took Sarah into his palace, intending to marry her. Hagar is believed to be among the servants he gave to Abraham.

> *Please say you are my sister, that it may be well with me for your sake, and that I may live because of you." So it was, when Abram came into Egypt, that the Egyptians saw the woman, that she was very beautiful. The princes of Pharaoh also saw her and commended her to Pharaoh. And the woman was taken to Pharaoh's house. He treated Abram well for her sake. He had sheep, oxen, male donkeys, male and female servants, female donkeys, and camels.*
> Genesis 12:12-16 (NKJV)

As I looked over Hagar's life, my heart went out to her. Her sadness and the rejection of her son, reminds me of the story of the beautiful young girl in chapter one. She had become so miserable in the wilderness, but God brought her to a wonderful, happy ending.

During the lifetime of our earlier ancestors, Abraham and Sarah, the Lord God Almighty promised them a son. Sarah wanted this child of promise so badly that she told her husband to take her servant girl, Hagar, as a wife so they could have a son through her. This was their custom if a wife couldn't have a child and is still the custom in many nations today. However, this is not God's custom. Some were even considered a disgrace among the women of that time if they couldn't bear children. But it was not considered a disgrace to the Lord. Others have said it was a curse from God. There were times when he would prevent a woman from giving birth until an appointed time, and there were times when he would shut a woman's womb as a sign of judgment due to sin. But whenever repentance was made, he would forgive and heal.

> *"The LORD has kept me from having any children," Sarai said to Abram. "Go and sleep with my servant. Perhaps I can have children through her." And Abram agreed.*
>
> Genesis 16:2 b (NLT)

Sometimes the women who were married with children would tease the women who were married and had no children. For example, this was the case with the woman named Peninnah. She teased Hannah because she had no children. The more she teased Hannah, the more Hannah cried. She wouldn't even eat.

> *Elkanah had two wives, Hannah and Peninnah. Peninnah had children, while Hannah did not. But Peninnah made fun of Hannah because the LORD had closed her womb. Year after year it was the same—Peninnah would taunt Hannah as they went to the Tabernacle. Hannah would finally be reduced to tears and would not even eat.*
>
> 1 Samuel 1:2, 6–7 (NLT)

Because of Hannah's overwhelming grief for her lack of a child, she went to the temple of Shiloh and cried to the Lord in prayer. She told the Lord that if he would give her a son, she would give him back to the Lord in service to him. The Lord saw all her tears, heard all her cries, and he answered her prayer. She gave birth to a son and named him Samuel.

> *So it came to pass in the process of time that Hannah conceived and bore a son, and called his name Samuel, saying, "Because I have asked for him from the Lord."*
>
> 1 Samuel 1:20 (NKJV)

Hannah means *grace*. Samuel means *the name is God* or *God is exalted*. It also means *Son of God*. The Lord showed his grace unto Hannah, and she gave her son back to God in service to him. The Lord used Samuel as a prophet to Israel. The Lord didn't stop with one child. He blessed her with three more sons and two daughters.

> *And the Lord visited Hannah, so that she conceived and bore three sons and two daughters. Meanwhile the child Samuel grew before the Lord.*
> 1 Samuel 2:21 (NKJV)

People often say, *Be careful what you pray for, you might get it!* I'd like to say, *Those you tease and trample down in life are the main ones who benefit from life!* I'd also like to add, *Be careful whom you mess with.* God made Hannah's son Samuel his spokesman to the nation of Israel. He was one of the greatest prophets who ever lived, and great was his reward and that of his mother. God honored Hannah by recording her grief, her prayer, her faith, her faithful vow, and praises to him in his book. The Lord was so pleased with Hannah's prayer of praise and thanksgiving to him for giving her a son, that he later gave her three more sons and two daughters. As for Peninnah and her children, there is nothing more said about any of them.

The Lord responds to all of our cries whenever times of sadness, loneliness, neglect, rejection, disappointments, troubles, or disaster strike our lives. Not one tear falls from our eyes and he not know it, even our tears of joy. Whenever I cry because of pain, trouble, or sorrow that visits my life or those I see in the world around me, I always think of Psalm 56:8 about how God records every one of our tears. The Lord is greatly moved by all of our tears and sorrows—so much so that he said one day he is going to do away with it all. Until then, we have to learn to trust and lean on him and know he loves and cares for us so very much. The more intimate we become with him, the more we will trust him and see his plan for our lives and how it will come into full bloom at the appointed time.

Sarah, I'm sure, was teased like Hannah too, throughout her marriage to Abraham. But it was not until she was about seventy-six years of age that the Lord told them they would have a son. Seeing that ten years had passed since the promise was given, she probably thought the only way for this to come true was to use one of her servant girls. And that's where Hagar came in.

Frankly, I could not bear the thought of my husband, the man I love and with whom I share sexual intimacy, lying with another woman, servant or not. Though that was their custom in those days as a method for having children when a wife was barren, it would tear my heart apart. What if it had taken several acts of sexual encounters before she became pregnant? What if, after he slept with her, she never became pregnant?

I believe at this time she was determined that they have a son, not just because she just had to have one, but to carry on the family lineage. Abraham and Sarah were accustomed to this method of bearing children, and they always had servants, but we don't see anywhere in the Scriptures where she asked Abraham to marry any of them until after the Lord told them they were going to have a son. I don't say this in disrespect for Sarah and Abraham because they are my ancestors, and it was through them I am able to receive the covenant blessings God promised him.

> *There is no longer Jew or Gentile, slave or free, male or female. For you are all Christians—you are one in Christ*

> Jesus. And now that you belong to Christ, you are the true children of Abraham. You are his heirs, and now all the promises God gave to him belong to you.
>
> Galatians 3:28–29 (NLT)

I realize that the law was not given then and that many women were treated like cattle. In fact, many are still treated that way today in many parts of the world. Because of sin in the human heart, these are the results of things that take place when people are not governed by righteous laws. Rather than do what is right for the other person or persons, people usually do what they think is right for self. That is why God gave us laws and statutes to live by. If what we think is right goes contrary to what God says is right, then which one of us do you guess is wrong?

> There is a way that seems right to a man, but its end is the way of death.
>
> Proverbs 14:12 (NKJV)

> Every way of a man is right in his own eyes, but the Lord weighs the hearts.
>
> Proverbs 21:2 (NKJV)

God, from the very beginning, never meant for a man to have more than one wife. Let's take a cruise back up the river to the beginning of creation for a few minutes here, and then we will cruise back over to the life of Hagar.

> And the Lord God caused a deep sleep to fall on Adam, and he slept; and He took one of his ribs, and closed up the flesh in its place. Then the rib which the LORD God had taken from man He made into a woman, and He brought her to the man. And Adam said: "This is now bone of my bones

and flesh of my flesh; she shall be called Woman, because she was taken out of Man." Therefore a man shall leave his father and mother and be joined to his wife, and they shall become one flesh. And they were both naked, the man and his wife, and were not ashamed.
Genesis 2:21–25 (NKJV)

God brought to the man one woman to be his wife. Not just a sex partner. Not a cohabitant. And it certainly was not another man. He brought him one woman to be his wife, to complement him. That was it! Not two or four or one hundred or one thousand. God didn't say: *Hey, Adam! Take a look at what I have for you—some women! And you can have as many as you want!* No, he brought to man one woman and told them, together, they are to become one flesh. And from the coming together of their one-flesh-ness, they are to multiply and bring forth more flesh (children). God created man and for him one wife, for life. He created them with a desire to know each other intimately in the purest form ever known to man. No man and woman can know intimacy on that level, unless they have been joined together by the Lord in holy matrimony and have a love that is pure and loyal towards each other. Anything apart from that is fornication, whore-mongering, adultery, and waiting the judgment of God if not repented of.

By the way! Have you ever wondered what sexual intimacy would have been like for Adam and Eve and what their children would have been like before they sinned in the garden? They had their first son, Cain, shortly after they were sent away from the Garden of Eden. Satan didn't waste any time. He knew what God was looking for—godly children—and Satan attacked their union, just like he is still doing today. He has no new tactics.

> *Didn't the Lord make you one with your wife? In body and spirit you are his. And what does he want? Godly children from your union. So guard yourself; remain loyal to the wife of your youth. "For I hate divorce!" says the Lord, the God of Israel. "It is as cruel as putting on a victim's bloodstained coat," says the Lord Almighty. "So guard yourself; always remain loyal to your wife."*
>
> Malachi 2:15–16 (NLT)

Job, a man after my own heart and one of the richest and wisest men who ever lived, understood this perfectly. He feared God and wouldn't have anything to do with evil. He understood the blessing of covenant marriage and the curse of lusting for other women. He understood that it was wrong for a man to desire another man's wife. In fact, he called it a crime that required punishing.

Job was so committed to God and his wife that he made a covenant with his own eyes that he would not look with lust after other women. Other translations said, a virgin, one said a maid, another said a girl. Job knew what lust could do to him and his relationship with God and his family, and he wasn't about to let any female, nor his flesh separate him from them.

> *I made a covenant with my eyes not to look with lust upon a young woman. What has God above chosen for us? What is our inheritance from the Almighty on high? It is calamity for the wicked, misfortune for those who do evil. He sees everything I do and every step I take.*
>
> Job 31:1–4 (NLT)

> *If my heart has been seduced by a woman, or if I have lusted for my neighbor's wife, then may my wife belong to another man; may other men sleep with her. For lust is a shameful sin, a crime that should be punished. It is a devastating fire that destroys to hell. It would wipe out everything I own.*
>
> Job 31:9–12 (NLT)

Job understood perfectly that all his wealth came from God. He knew God had given him his wife and his children. He knew the punishment for sin, and he knew God saw his every move. And he was completely devoted to God and serving others with an upright heart. No wonder God said there was no other man like him in all the earth. What a testimony.

> *And the Lord said unto Satan, "Hast thou considered my servant Job, that there is none like him in the earth, a perfect and an upright man, one that feareth God, and escheweth evil?"*
>
> Job 1:8 (KJV)

Job hated evil and he knew lust failed in that category. I have had men say to me they "love" women and "have a weakness" for women. The problem is not love for women. There is nothing wrong with loving women. It is perfectly natural for men to love women. Love is providing for, protection, and even dying for. Love is simply doing what is right. The problem is not love. The problem is lust. That is evil. Lust will cause one to be unfaithful to a spouse. Lust will rob you of your bank account. Lust will lie rather than tell the truth. Lust would beat and even kill you. Lust will steal from your children rather than provide for them. All this happens when men and women love evil, unlike Job, who hated evil. Because of Job's integrity and his faith in God, when he was tested and lost all he had, God restored it all in a double portion. Talk about doubling your earnings.

> *And the Lord restored Job's losses when he prayed for his friends. Indeed the Lord gave Job twice as much as he had before.*
>
> Job 42:10 (NKJV)

He knew it was wrong for a man to be unfaithful to God by sinning against him or other people. He even spoke of our ancestor Adam by saying he did not transgress as Adam had done in disobeying God.

> *If I covered my transgressions as Adam, by hiding mine iniquity in my bosom: Did I fear a great multitude, or did the contempt of families terrify me, that I kept silence, and went not out of the door? Oh that one would hear me! Behold, my desire is, that the Almighty would answer me, and that mine adversary had written a book.*
>
> Job 31:33–35 (KJV)

And as you can also see, a book was written about Job, but not by his adversary, but by the Almighty in honor of Job's reverence for God, because he was right about God, unlike his three friends. They accused him of living sinfully when he was tested by Satan, but the Lord vindicated Job.

> *After the Lord had finished speaking to Job, he said to Eliphaz the Temanite: "I am angry with you and with your two friends, for you have not been right in what you said about me, as my servant Job was."*
>
> Job 42:7 (NLT)

Job loved righteousness and he loved his wife, their children, and people. Yes, Job is definitely a man after my own heart. Oh, if only we had more men like Job in our generation today. Scandals in Washington, in corporate America, Hollywood, and yes, even in the churches, would be few and far between. Divorce and single mothers left to raise their children alone would decrease. Children would grow up happier, more stable, and flourishing in life, having both loving parents raising them in the home.

Adam, meaning *man*, declared that woman was bone of his bone and flesh of his flesh, and then he named her *wo-man*. She was also called Eve, meaning *life*, or *mother of all living*. And God was very pleased.

> *"At last!" Adam exclaimed. "She is part of my own flesh and bone! She will be called woman, because she was taken out of man." This explains why a man leaves his father and mother and is joined to his wife, and the two are united into one.*
> Genesis 2:23–24 (NLT)

Adam named everything, including his wife. That is the way God wanted it because he gave him the authority. God gave him his woman as a helpmate. Before Adam sinned in the Garden of Eden, he functioned at 100 percent of his brainpower. But now scientific study shows that a *genius* operates at 8 to 10 percent of his brainpower. Hey now! Where does that leave you? Just kidding!

> *So the Lord God formed from the soil every kind of animal and bird. He brought them to Adam to see what he would call them, and Adam chose a name for each one. He gave names to all the livestock, birds, and wild animals. But still there was no companion suitable for him.*
> Genesis 2:19–20 (NLT)

Some of you are thinking, *Well, what about men in the Bible like Solomon, who had seven hundred wives and three hundred concubines?* Well, God was not pleased with it. God warned Solomon beforehand about that and how these women would turn his heart from him to false gods. Nevertheless, in his old age, he disobeyed God, and as a result, he lost the kingdom, but not to one of his sons, instead to a servant. It was after his death that the kingdom split. And there was no longer peace in the land.

These are the kind of things that happen when the eyes of man are never satisfied. You have to make yourself be content, or you could lose everything you have. God is a God of unity, not division, and disobedience always brings division, and division brings trouble, and trouble, sorrow. These things rob us of our peace, joy, and prosperity.

It was not the color of the skin that the Lord was concerned about, as some think; it was because the people of the other nations worshiped false gods, man-made idols, and all the kind of things the Lord detests. He did not want the children of Israel to be influenced to practice such sins.

> *The Lord had clearly instructed his people not to intermarry with those nations, because the women they married would lead them to worship their gods. Yet Solomon when he grew old, insisted on loving these women anyway. He had seven hundred wives and three hundred concubines. And sure enough, they led his heart away from the Lord.*
> 1 Kings 11:2–3 (NLT)

> *The Lord was very angry with Solomon, for his heart had turned away from the Lord, the God of Israel, who had appeared to him twice. He had warned Solomon specifically about worshiping other gods, but Solomon did not listen to the Lord's command. So now the Lord said to him, "Since you have not kept my covenant and have disobeyed my laws, I will surely tear the kingdom away from you and give it to one of your servants."*
> 1 Kings 11:9–11 (NLT)

It's something about a man when he is old to thinks he's still young and still got it. Though he may still have it, what makes him want to give up a woman who has given herself to him all her life to pursue something young and something new? Or should I say used! God hates that, and just like Solomon, who didn't get away with it, neither will the husband who is disloyal to his wife. That goes for a wife too.

> *You cry out, "Why has the* L*ORD* *abandoned us?" I'll tell you why! Because the* L*ORD* *witnessed the vows you and your wife made to each other on your wedding day when you were young. But you have been disloyal to her, though she remained your faithful companion, the wife of your marriage vows. Didn't the* L*ORD* *make you one with your wife? In body and spirit you are his. And what does he want? Godly children from your union. So guard yourself; remain loyal to the wife of your youth. "For I hate divorce!" says the* L*ORD, the God of Israel. "It is as cruel as putting on a victim's bloodstained coat," says the* L*ORD* *Almighty. "So guard yourself; always remain loyal to your wife."*
> Malachi 2:14–16 (NLT)

Again, from the beginning of creation, God created one man and one woman—not one man and many women. After the fall of the human race, man started taking for himself more than one woman to be his wife. The first man to take on two wives was Lamech, a descendant of Adam's first son, Cain. Again I say, the Lord never meant for a man to have more than one woman. Man came up with that idea when sin entered the earth through the temptation of Satan. Adam had one wife. Then their first son, Cain, meaning *I have created*, went to live in the city of Nod, meaning *wandering*. This was after God told him he would become a wanderer on the earth and that the earth would not yield to the work of his hands. He was then banished from God's presence because he killed his brother

Abel, just like his parents were banished from the Garden of Eden when they ate the forbidden fruit.

But the Lord gave Adam and Eve a third son and they named him Seth, meaning *he set, appointed,* or *replacement.* God appointed Seth to be the lineage through which the Messiah would come, and he was Abel's replacement. He couldn't use Cain because his spirit was not right. He had blood on his hands.

Five generations later, a descendant of Cain named Lamech married two women. These things were done because of sin, and no laws had been given at that time. It appears that Lamech started this more-than-one-wife business.

> *Then Cain went out from the presence of the Lord and dwelt in the land of Nod on the east of Eden. And Cain knew his wife, and she conceived and bore Enoch. And he built a city, and called the name of the city after the name of his son—Enoch. To Enoch was born Irad; and Irad begot Mehujael, and Mehujael begot Methushael, and Methushael begot Lamech.*
>
> Genesis 4:16–18 (NKJV)

> *Lamech married two women—Adah and Zillah.*
>
> Genesis 4:19 (NLT)

> *One day Lamech said to Adah and Zillah, "Listen to me, my wives. I have killed a youth who attacked and wounded me. If anyone who kills Cain is to be punished seven times, anyone who takes revenge against me will be punished seventy-seven times."*
>
> Genesis 4:23–24 (NLT)

Adam, who is also called the first Adam, disobeyed the word of God, which stated that he was not to eat from the tree of the knowledge of good and evil, breaking fellowship with God. This opened the door to poverty, sickness, death, disease, and violence, which included an unforgiving or avenging spirit. Lamech told his two wives that anyone who tried to take revenge against him, he declared punishment on them seventy-seven times, but Jesus came to undo that. He told Peter we are to forgive seventy times seven, in a day. That's 490 times in a day.

> *Then Peter came to him and asked, "Lord, how often should I forgive someone who sins against me? Seven times?" "No," Jesus replied, "seventy times seven."*
> Matthew 18:21–22 (NLT)

Now, let's go back to tent of Abraham and Hagar. Abraham did as Sarah suggested and took Hagar as his second wife and then had sexual intercourse with her, and she became pregnant. I have often wondered how Hagar must have felt to be given as a wife to Abraham and have intercourse with Abraham just so she could bear a child for him and Sarah. No passion, no emotional bonding, or tender loving intimacy that a loving couple normally shares. Just intercourse! I can just hear some women saying, "Hey, that's cool with me, just as long as he remains my sugar daddy!" Well, this next verse is definitely the one for you.

> *Marriage is honorable among all, and the bed undefiled; but fornicators and adulterers God will judge.*
> Hebrews 13:4 (NKJV)

> *So Sarai, Abram's wife, took Hagar the Egyptian servant and gave her to Abram as a wife. (This happened ten years after Abram first arrived in the land of Canaan.) So Abram slept with Hagar, and she became pregnant.*
> Genesis 16:3–4b (NLT)

For a woman, slave or free, this is not an easy task and can cause permanent emotional and spiritual damage. Then to carry a child for nine months and hand him over as if he were just a piece of meat is heartbreaking, and yet many times this side of the story has been overlooked, but not by the Lord.

Not only that, how could they have guaranteed that the baby would be a son? The baby could have been a daughter. What if they have to keep trying over and over again until a son was born? Now that could have really gotten messy. But God foresaw the life of Hagar from beginning to ending, and he had his own plan for her life too.

The Sovereign God predetermines what will be in the womb and preplans his or her life's destiny. The Lord told Hagar what to name her son and that he was going to make of her son a great nation.

> *And the angel also said, "You are now pregnant and will give birth to a son. You are to name him Ishmael, for the Lord has heard about your misery. This son of yours will be a wild one—free and untamed as a wild donkey! He will be against everyone, and everyone will be against him. Yes, he will live at odds with the rest of his brothers."*
>
> *Thereafter, Hagar referred to the* Lord, *who had spoken to her, as the God who sees me, for she said, "I have seen the One who sees me!" Later that well was named Beer-lahairoi, and it can still be found between Kadesh and Bered. So Hagar gave Abram a son, and Abram named him Ishmael.*
>
> Genesis 16:11–15 (NLT)

> *And as for Ishmael, I have heard you. Behold, I have blessed him, and will make him fruitful, and will multiply him exceedingly. He shall beget twelve princes, and I will make him a great nation.*
>
> Genesis 17:20 (NKJV)

While Hagar was pregnant, she began to despise Sarah. Seeing her dilemma, one can certainly understand why. Her response was rather natural for a woman knowing that she was taken and given to sleep with another woman's husband just so she could be impregnated for her. Hagar had probably felt that she was better than Sarah because she was able to give birth. But now she would carry the baby for nine months and then have to give the baby up. Feeling him move inside of her, nurturing the baby, bonding with him, then to bring the baby forth through childbearing pain and have to give him up was probably tormenting her. It probably angered her to realize she would never be able to claim the child as her own.

When we fail to rely on the spoken word of God to us and we put our trust in flesh (that is, mankind), we can really make a mess of things. The descendants of Ishmael and Isaac are still at odds with each other in the Middle East because of the decision Abraham made. It looks as though these brothers got their attitude of opposition from their mothers.

I am sure we all can think of decisions we have made because we trusted in the flesh of ourselves or another, rather than the Spirit of God and caused confusion and chaos in our lives or the lives of others. It is very foolish to believe that the decisions we make do not affect other people. It always has been foolish, and it always will be. In fact, it would be wise of us to make our decisions based on how they will affect others rather than for ourselves. This is a principle of love.

The actions of Abraham and Sarah did not catch God by surprise. God named Hagar's son and decreed to bless him and make of him a great nation also. Even though the descendants of these two women are still at odds with each other today, God is not through with them. Remember, Ishmael's name means *God hears*. That was not just presently speaking but prophetically speaking as well. God will hear their cry in the wilderness in the days to come.

God promised Abraham that through his seed Isaac, the Messiah would come, but he also told him all the family of the earth would be blessed through him. No matter who we are, if we repent, God will forgive and bless us. And to the descendants of Ishmael, should any of them repent, God will forgive them too. However, God said to Abraham, as for his everlasting covenant promise, it is through Isaac.

Sometimes I feel we may be missing a part of the picture concerning Ishmael, because he is Abraham's son too, and God promised to bless him because Abraham asked him to. God saved Lot when Abraham asked him, and just because Abraham is not here on earth doesn't stop him from talking to God about his family. He's just doing it in another location.

Even though these descendants were at each other's throats, I believe God still has a plan. Remember, there are things God has revealed to us, and there are things he keeps for himself. For example, we all know that the heavenly Father will bring an end to all sin and corruption, but Jesus even said he does not know the time appointed. Only the heavenly Father knows that.

Abraham and Sarah's actions were not God's perfect will or order. This brought about confusion and conflict. God is not the author of confusion, but he is a God of peace. However, he will use our mistakes and still bring about his own plans and perfect will. He will take the confusion and bring peace for his glory and his namesake.

> *For God is not a God of disorder, but of peace.*
> 1 Corinthians 14:33a (NLT)

Sarah blamed Abraham for the way Hagar behaved toward her. And Abraham told Sarah to do as she pleased with Hagar because she was her handmaid. So, Sarah did just that. Sarah was very harsh with Hagar, causing Hagar to run away.

> *And when Sarai dealt severely with her, humbling and afflicting her, she (Hagar) fled from her. But the Angel of the Lord found her by a spring of water in the wilderness on the road of Shur. And He said, Hagar, Sarai's maid, where did come from and where are you intending to go? And she said, I am running away from my mistress Sarai. The Angel of the Lord said to her, Go back to your mistress and (humbly) submit to her control. Also the Angel of the Lord said to her, I will multiply your descendants exceedingly so that they shall not be numbered for multitudes. And the Angel continued, See now you are with child and shall bare a son and shall call his name Ishmael (God hears), because the Lord has heard and paid attention to your affliction.*
> Genesis 16:6b–11 (AMP)

Now, just where do you think she was going? There she was this little rose in blossom and just weeks away from giving birth to what was sure to be a son now. I guess at that time in her life it didn't matter where she was going. She had had enough. She was already a slave girl, servant to Sarah; then made to be another wife to Abraham, just so she could have a baby for them. She was treated harshly by Sarah because she got an attitude about it. One translation says she was beaten while pregnant. Hagar was miserable and was probably trying to go home to her family and all those she knew back in Egypt. She had become a stranger in a strange land. I'm sure she wanted to go back home to her own homeland with hopes of having children of her own and a husband who would love her like Abraham loved Sarah.

When you are angry, hurt, frighten and unhappy, all kind of thoughts goes through your mind. If Hagar was one of the servants given to Abraham, she may have asked herself, why me? What have I done? Does this God, whom this people speak so much about, not care about me? Why would he allow me to be taken from my people, to a land among strangers whom I know nothing about? Why didn't Abraham tell Pharaoh the truth about his wife Sarah? Then I would still be at home, in my own land, among my own people. Was I no longer good enough to serve in the house of Pharaoh? When this God whom they speak of punished Pharaoh, why didn't he set me free? In all actually, the Lord did. The Lord saw her future, but all she could see was her past, her present and her pain, like so many of us. The Lord saw Hagar, before Abraham ever arrived. Who knows what things she made have cried about as a young girl. Though she was once a slave girl, she is now the mother of a nation still in the news today. They are the Arab nation and brothers to the nation of Israel, whom I pray will repent too and be united with them in Christ.

It is the Lord who charts our course in life. Even when we get off course, he knows how to steer us back. Many times the roads we take are a part of the Lord's plan for us. Abraham's course, lead him to Egypt due to a famine in the land. He thought the men of city were ungodly, and once they saw how beautiful Sarah was, they would try to kill him for her. Sure enough, Pharaoh took her. This incident caused the Lord to judge Pharaoh. God set a plague on his entire house. However, God showed him mercy because Pharaoh didn't know she was Abraham's wife. He returned Sarah to Abraham as fast as he could and sent them away, along with an abundant of cattle and servants. Ah ha! The Lord saw an opportune time to prosper Abraham during the time of famine. And he knew just where to get it.

> *"Therefore it will happen, when the Egyptians see you, that they will say, 'This is his wife;' and they will kill me, but they will let you live. Please say you are my sister, that it may be well with me for your sake, and that I may live because of you." So it was, when Abram came into Egypt, that the Egyptians saw the woman, that she was very beautiful. The princes of Pharaoh also saw her and commended her to Pharaoh. And the woman was taken to Pharaoh's house. He treated Abram well for her sake. He had sheep, oxen, male donkeys, male and female servants, female donkeys, and camels. But the Lord plagued Pharaoh and his house with great plagues because of Sarai, Abram's wife. And Pharaoh called Abram and said, "What is this you have done to me? Why did you not tell me that she was your wife? Why did you say, 'She is my sister'? I might have taken her as my wife. Now therefore, here is your wife; take her and go your way." So Pharaoh commanded his men concerning him; and they sent him away, with his wife and all that he had.*
> Genesis 12:12–20 (NKJV)

You know, I used to wonder why the Lord got so angry with Pharaoh and set a plague upon the women of his house, since he had been led to believe Sarah was Abraham's sister. Then I realized it's because the Lord hates adultery and that is why he was angry with him. Pharaoh had plenty wives, and his greed for another woman, all because she was so beautiful, aroused the Lord's anger, because this time she was another man's wife.

Even though the law was not given yet, the people knew subconsciously, what is right and what is wrong. Pharaoh didn't know anything about Moses and the Ten Commandments, because Moses had not been born yet. We know subconsciously and we have the law and yet our generation acts far worst then them. Unlike a lot of men and women in our generation today, this Pharaoh had a conscience that feared God and he was keenly aware of the danger of committing adultery.

If men and women feared God today like this Pharaoh and many others in his day, we would not hear all of the things splashed all over the media today—things such as a president committing adultery on the highest land and in the highest office in the nation, or a senator being arrested for misdemeanor disorderly conduct in a men's restroom, or a mayor's love affair with his chief of staff, or a governor having to resign due to a prostitution scandal, or a governor having a love affair with another woman, claiming she is his soul mate.

Any time you have sex with someone, your souls mate. You become one with that person and every individual that person has mated with. It's called *soul ties*. Sexual immorality over a period time destroys marriages, distorts one's ability to make good judgment, and destroys the soul, the body, and eventually your life. The Lord hates what adultery and all forms of sexual immorality do to people. That is why he warns us in his Word not to practice it. God honors marriage, not lust and sexual immorality.

> *If my heart has been seduced by a woman, or if I have lusted for my neighbor's wife, then may my wife belong to another man; may other men sleep with her. For lust is a shameful sin, a crime that should be punished. It is a devastating fire that destroys to hell. It would wipe out everything I own.*
>
> Job 31:9–12 (NLT)

> *Run away from sexual sin! No other sin so clearly affects the body as this one does. For sexual immorality is a sin against your own body.*
>
> 1 Corinthians 6:18 (NLT)

When the Lord showed Abimelech that Sarah was married, he couldn't get out of bed fast enough to make things right with God, Abraham and Sarah. With great fear he expressed to Abraham how he felt about it. He questioned Abraham, gave Sarah back to him and paid him greatly for their trouble. And, unlike Pharaoh, king of Egypt, whom God judged for taking Sarah too, returned her back to Abraham and then he had them escorted out of his land (Genesis 12:17-20), Abimelech, king of Gerar, told Abraham, to choose whatever part of his kingdom he wanted for them to live.

> *"You are a dead man, for that woman you took is married." But Abimelech had not slept with her yet, so he said, "Lord, will you kill an innocent man? Abraham told me, 'She is my sister,' and she herself said, 'Yes, he is my brother.' I acted in complete innocence!" "Yes, I know you are innocent," God replied. "That is why I kept you from sinning against me; I did not let you touch her. Now return her to her husband, and he will pray for you, for he is a prophet. Then you will live. But if you don't return her to him, you can be sure that you and your entire household will die." Abimelech got up early the next morning and hastily called a meeting of all his servants. When he told them what had happened, great fear swept through the crowd. Then Abimelech called for Abraham. "What is this you have done to us?" he demanded. "What have I done to you that deserves treatment like this, making me and my kingdom guilty of this great sin? This kind of thing should not be done! Why have you done this to us?" "Then Abimelech took sheep and oxen and servants— both men and women—and gave them to Abraham, and he returned his wife, Sarah, to him. "Look over my kingdom, and choose a place where you would like to live," Abimelech told him. Then he turned to Sarah. "Look," he said, "I am giving your 'brother' a thousand pieces of silver to compensate for any embarrassment I may have caused you. This will*

settle any claim against me in this matter." Then Abraham prayed to God, and God healed Abimelech, his wife, and the other women of the household, so they could have children. For the L*ORD* *had stricken all the women with infertility as a warning to Abimelech for having taken Abraham's wife.*

Genesis 20:3-18 (NLT)

God was about to kill him over Sarah. If she had been a free woman, it would have been accepted. But Sarah was Abraham's wife and God hates adultery. King David angered the Lord because he slept with Bathsheba, Uriah's wife. Had Uriah died and then David pursued her to be his wife, it would not have angered the Lord. The Lord did not get angry with David when he took Abigail for a wife because her husband, Nabal, had died. David committed adultery with Bathsheba, had her husband killed, and then married her.

Marriage is wonderful, but adultery is dangerously sinful. When David realized he had sinned and angered the Lord, he repented quickly. And the Lord forgave him, but he still reaped the consequences.

> *Then Nathan said to David, "You are the man! Thus says the Lord God of Israel: 'I anointed you king over Israel, and I delivered you from the hand of Saul. I gave you your master's house and your master's wives into your keeping, and gave you the house of Israel and Judah. And if that had been too little, I also would have given you much more! Why have you despised the commandment of the Lord, to do evil in His sight? You have killed Uriah the Hittite with the sword; you have taken his wife to be your wife, and have killed him with the sword of the people of Ammon. Now therefore, the sword shall never depart from your house, because you have despised Me, and have taken the wife of Uriah the Hittite to be your wife.' Thus says the*

> *Lord: 'Behold, I will raise up adversity against you from your own house; and I will take your wives before your eyes and give them to your neighbor, and he shall lie with your wives in the sight of this sun. For you did it secretly, but I will do this thing before all Israel, before the sun.'"*
> 2 Samuel 12:7–12 (NKJV)

> *But the man who commits adultery is an utter fool, for he destroys his own soul.*
> Proverbs 6:32 (NLT)

Fellas, if you're going to sleep with someone, you better make sure she's not someone else's wife, but yours alone. If you don't, the Lord God is sure to pay a visit to your house. Some of you might be in trouble right now as a result of this very act, but never made the connection. Repent! The Lord will forgive you and even restore what needs restoring.

> *For the Lord sees clearly what a man does, examining every path he takes. An evil man is held captive by his own sins; they are ropes that catch and hold him. He will die for lack of self-control; he will be lost because of his incredible folly.*
> Proverbs 5:21–23 (NLT)

Let's get back to Hagar. The Lord saw all of Hagar's misery. He was moved by her pain and sorrow and came to comfort her. He appeared to her and told her to go back to Sarah and submit to her and promised to bless her son. She obeyed him and went back to Sarah and submitted herself. At this time, she knew there was a real and living God who hears and responds to our cries.

Later, after Ishmael and Isaac were both born, Ishmael kept picking on Isaac, and Sarah couldn't stand neither him nor his mother. So she told Abraham to send them away. But this time he wouldn't listen to Sarah. Then the Lord spoke with him and said to do what Sarah said. God had made a promise to Hagar to bless her and her son, and the time had come to do so.

> *As time went by and Isaac grew and was weaned, Abraham gave a big party to celebrate the happy occasion. But Sarah saw Ishmael—the son of Abraham and her Egyptian servant Hagar—making fun of Isaac. So she turned to Abraham and demanded, "Get rid of that servant and her son. He is not going to share the family inheritance with my son, Isaac. I won't have it!" This upset Abraham very much because Ishmael was his son.*
>
> *But God told Abraham, "Do not be upset over the boy and your servant wife. Do just as Sarah says, for Isaac is the son through whom your descendants will be counted. But I will make a nation of the descendants of Hagar's son because he also is your son." So Abraham got up early the next morning, prepared food for the journey, and strapped a container of water to Hagar's shoulders. He sent her away with their son, and she walked out into the wilderness of Beersheba, wandering aimlessly.*
>
> Genesis 21:8–14 (NLT)

Food for their journey and a container of water! That's it? No money? No caravan? No servants to help them and protect them? I can sense the look of fear, anger, and misery on her face and in her heart, while everyone just watched as she and her son walked off into the hot, desert sun. They had nothing but the clothes on their back, just enough food to last on the journey, and a container of water.

Hagar wandered through that wilderness until she ran completely out of water. She had lost her life back in Egypt. She lost her security among the tents of Abraham, and now she was about to lose her son. She had forgotten the promise that the Lord gave her back at the well when she first ran away from Sarah. She had lost faith, just like many of us do. For years, she had served Abraham and Sarah and was made to have a child for them. Now she and her fourteen-year-old son had been thrown away. Just like that! But remember, the Lord God Almighty had a plan, and he again stepped right in.

> *When the water was gone, she left the boy in the shade of a bush. Then she went and sat down by herself about a hundred yards away. "I don't want to watch the boy die," she said, as she burst into tears. Then God heard the boy's cries, and the angel of God called to Hagar from the sky, "Hagar, what's wrong? Do not be afraid!*
>
> *God has heard the boy's cries from the place where you laid him. Go to him and comfort him, for I will make a great nation from his descendants." Then God opened Hagar's eyes, and she saw a well. She immediately filled her water container and gave the boy a drink. And God was with the boy as he grew up in the wilderness of Paran. He became an expert archer, and his mother arranged a marriage for him with a young woman from Egypt.*
>
> Genesis 21:15–21 (NLT)

> *Now this is the genealogy of Ishmael, Abraham's son, whom Hagar the Egyptian, Sarah's maidservant, bore to Abraham. And these were the names of the sons of Ishmael, by their names, according to their generations: The firstborn of Ishmael, Nebajoth; then Kedar, Adbeel, Mibsam, Mishma, Dumah, Massa, Hadar, Tema, Jetur, Naphish, and Kedemah.*
>
> *These were the sons of Ishmael and these were their names, by their towns and their settlements, twelve princes according to their nations.*
>
> Genesis 25:12–16 (NKJV)

I just love happy endings. Don't you? Now I don't mean any harm here, but, when did God leave him? The word says God was with Ishmael as grew up. Hagar obeyed the Lord and returned to Sarah and delivered her baby, and God kept his promise to her. She was taken from Egypt as a slave, but the Lord carried her back home and kept his promise to her. Hagar became a very happy and rich grandmother of twelve grand-princes (twelve grandsons) through Ishmael. At God's appointed time!

God is a good God and a God of justice. He is a God who hears and answers our cries. He not only knows our past, but our present and future too. He is the one who calls it. God knew what Hagar was to undergo before it happened. He revealed to her what gender of child she was going to have. Gave him the name Ishmael (*God hears*) and declared the child's future. All of this the Lord told her before the child was born.

Hagar's flight into the desert sun brought her down upon her knees, and that is the place her life took on a whole new direction. God gave her a word concerning her life's destiny and the destiny of her son and his descendants.

> *"For I know the plans I have for you," says the Lord. "They are plans for good and not for disaster, to give you a future and a hope."*
>
> Jeremiah 29:11 (NLT)

Sometimes we, or others, can make a mess of our lives, but God knows just how to clean it up. You might be in a bad situation somewhat like Hagar, or perhaps you know someone else who is. No matter whatever the case maybe. I want to encourage your hearts to let you know, God is no respecter of person. What he did for her, he will do for you. But be sure you are not rebelling against his word. That would be the very thing that will keep you from the blessings.

Perhaps he has told you to do something. Do it. Maybe he has given you a specific promise just for you; wait for the fulfillment of it. Perhaps the Lord has spoken a word concerning your future a few years ago and you, like Hagar, forgot. What word has he spoken to you concerning your present situation? It may have been ten or more years ago, doesn't matter. God has an appointed time for everyone and everything, even for the wicked.

> *God shall judge the righteous and the wicked, for there is a time there for every purpose and for every work.*
> Ecclesiastes 3:17b (NKJV)

> *For the vision is yet for an appointed time; but at the end it will speak, and it will not lie. Though it tarries, wait for it; because it will surely come, it will not tarry.*
> Habakkuk 2:3 (NKJV)

God showed Joseph, a grandson of Abraham, in a dream when he was seventeen that his family would bow before him. However, it did not come to pass until about sixteen years later. The Lord God took him from prison in Egypt and placed him second in command next to Pharaoh in a day. When his brothers came to Egypt, they bowed low before him. At the appointed time, it happened just as God said.

> *Now Joseph was governor over the land; and it was he who sold to all the people of the land. And Joseph's brothers came and bowed down before him with their faces to the earth. Joseph saw his brothers and recognized them, but he acted as a stranger to them and spoke roughly to them. Then he said to them, "Where do you come from?" And they said, "From*

> *the land of Canaan to buy food."* So Joseph recognized his brothers, but they did not recognize him. Then Joseph remembered the dreams which he had dreamed about them, and said to them, *"You are spies! You have come to see the nakedness of the land!"*
>
> Genesis 42:6–9 (NKJV)

Abraham was seventy-five when God promised to make of him a great nation. And he was one hundred and Sarah was ninety when Isaac was born. At the appointed time, it happened just as God said.

God told Abraham that for four hundred years, his descendants would be in bitter bondage in Egypt, but he would surely bring them out. God raised up a man named Moses, in the very house of Pharaoh of Egypt, four hundred years later. God used Moses and a staff to bring them out. At the appointed time, it happened just as God said.

I believe all this Hagar went through could have been avoided if Abraham had strongly reaffirmed and assured Sarah that God would fulfill his promise to them no matter how long it took. God promised Abraham in Genesis 12, when he was in the land of his brother Haran that he was going to bless him and make him a great man. He was told to leave this land and go to the land he would give him.

> *Then the Lord told Abram, "Leave your country. Your relatives and your father's house and go to the land that I will show you. I will cause you to become the father of a great nation. I will bless you and make your name great.*
>
> Genesis 12:1–2 (NLT)

Then the Lord came to him when he was in the land of Canaan, and there he told Abraham that Canaan and all the surrounding land, he was giving to him and his descendants.

> *Then the Lord appeared to Abram and said, "I am going to give this land to your offspring." And Abram built an altar there to commemorate the LORD's visit. After that, Abram traveled southward and set up camp in the hill country between Bethel on the west and Ai on the east. There he built an altar and worshiped the LORD. Then Abram traveled south by stages toward the Negev.*
> Genesis 12: 7–9 (NLT)

The Lord again appeared to Abraham in Genesis 13 and told him when he was in the hill country between Bethel and Ai, in every direction as far as he could see he was giving all that land to him and his descendants as a *permanent possession.*

> *After Lot was gone, the Lord said to Abram, "Look as far as you can see in every direction. I am going to give all this land to you and your offspring as a permanent possession. And I am going to give you so many descendants that, like dust, they cannot be counted! Take a walk in every direction and explore the new possessions I am giving you." Then Abram moved his camp to the oak grove owned by Mamre, which is at Hebron. There he built an altar to the Lord.*
> Genesis 13:14–18 (NLT)

Again, the Lord appeared to Abraham in Genesis 15 and reaffirmed to him all he was going to do for him. It was at this visitation that he promised him a son through his wife, Sarah. By this time, Abraham wanted proof, and God made a covenant with him right then and there. The Lord gave him his proof, sealing it with a blood covenant. Four times the Lord came to Abraham and told him all that he was going to do.

But ten years had passed. I guess Abraham had grown weary and yielded to the words of Sarah and his flesh.

> *But Abram replied "O Sovereign Lord, how can I be sure that you will give it to me?"*
> *Then the* LORD *told him, "Bring me a three-year-old heifer, a three-year-old female goat, a three-year-old ram, a turtledove, and a young pigeon." Abram took all these and killed them. He cut each one down the middle and laid the halves side by side. He did not, however, divide the birds in half. Some vultures came down to eat the carcasses, but Abram chased them away. That evening, as the sun was going down, Abram fell into a deep sleep. He saw a terrifying vision of darkness and horror. Then the* LORD *told Abram, "You can be sure that your descendants will be strangers in a foreign land, and they will be oppressed as slaves for four hundred years. But I will punish the nation that enslaves them, and in the end they will come away with great wealth. (But you will die in peace, at a ripe old age.) After four generations your descendants will return here to this land, when the sin of the Amorites has run its course. "As the sun went down and it became dark, Abram saw a smoking firepot and a flaming torch pass between the halves of the carcasses. So the* LORD *made a covenant with Abram that day and said, "I have given this land to your descendants, all the way from the border of Egypt to the great Euphrates River the land of the Kenites, Kenizzites, Kadmonites, Hittites, Perizzites, Rephaites, Amorites, Canaanites, Girgashites, and Jebusites."*
> Genesis 15:8–21 (NLT)

Well, God said it, and that settled it! But why didn't Sarah have enough faith to wait for the promise? Is it possible that Sarah didn't believe because Abraham failed to help her to see it? Or did she just grow impatient seeing now that ten years had passed and still they had no son? I believe that Abraham, being human, had failed to assure her of God's promise that they together were going to have a son.

All this started in Genesis chapter twelve, but we are going to sail over to chapter seventeen and chapter eighteen to see why Sarah had doubts. By this time, Ishmael was thirteen years of age. The Lord again confirmed his promise with Abraham, only this time he had to make an adjustment to that promise. You see, in Genesis chapters twelve up to sixteen, the Lord had promised to make him the father of *a great nation*. Single! But now Ishmael, Abraham's son by Hagar, was in the picture, so he had to make an adjustment to his promise. Now he is going to make Abraham the father of *nations*. Plural! In Genesis twelve, the Lord said:

> *I will cause you to become the father of a great nation.*
> Genesis 12:2a (NLT)

But now in Genesis chapter seventeen, the Lord had to make an amendment in addition to his first promise when he appeared to Abraham.

> *This is my covenant with you: I will make you the father of not just one nation, but a multitude of nations! What's more, I am changing your name. It will no longer be Abram; now you will be known as Abraham, for you will be the father of many nations. I will give you millions of descendants who will represent many nations. Kings will be among them! I will continue this everlasting covenant between us, generation after generation. It will continue between me and your offspring forever. And I will always be your God and the God of your descendants after you.*

> *Yes, I will give all this land of Canaan to you and to your offspring forever. And I will be their God.*
> Genesis 17:4–8 (NLT)

The Lord was constantly reminding Abraham of his promise to bless him. Right before the promise was manifested he changed their names. This change of names pulled them right into their destiny. This is why names should not be taken lightly or words used irresponsibly. We should name our children with purpose, not just because it sounds cute. And we should be careful how we speak concerning others and ourselves because our words are powerful. God warns us to be watchful of what we say.

God always keeps his word, and he does it at his appointed time. Thirteen years had passed since Ishmael was born, and the Lord had not spoken to Abraham. Now that the time was drawing near and the Lord having revisited Abraham concerning his promise, gave Sarah a new named too.

> *Then God added, "Regarding Sarai, your wife—her name will no longer be Sarai; from now on you will call her Sarah. And I will bless her and give you a son from her! Yes, I will bless her richly, and she will become the mother of many nations. Kings will be among her descendants!" Then Abraham bowed down to the ground, but he laughed to himself in disbelief. "How could I become a father at the age of one hundred?" he wondered. "Besides, Sarah is ninety; how could she have a baby?" And Abraham said to God, "Yes, may Ishmael enjoy your special blessing!" But God replied, "Sarah, your wife, will bear you a son. You will name him Isaac, and I will confirm my everlasting covenant with him and his descendants. As for Ishmael, I will bless him also, just as you have asked. I will cause him to multiply and become a great nation. Twelve princes will be among*

> his descendants. But my covenant is with Isaac, who will be born to you and Sarah about this time next year." That ended the conversation, and God left Abraham.
>
> Genesis 17:15–22 (NLT)

Well, now it looks like we had just pinpointed the place. I love this passage of scriptures and how the Lord addressed Abraham, after he responded saying, "Oh that Ishmael might live before you!" The Lord said, "No." I can just imagine Abraham on his face laughing and the Lord looking at him with a reserve expression on his face as if to say, "Oh you think that's funny huh?" Abraham thought they were too old. The Lord said what he had to say and left. Apparently Abraham believed the Lord, because that same day, when he got through laughing, he, Ishmael and his household were circumcised just as the Lord told him. Though the word of God says Abraham was strengthened in his faith and believed God, why wasn't Sarah?

> *That ended the conversation, and God left Abraham. On that very day Abraham took his son Ishmael and every other male in his household and circumcised them, cutting off their foreskins, exactly as God had told him. Abraham was ninety-nine years old at the time, and Ishmael his son was thirteen. Both were circumcised the same day, along with all the other men and boys of the household, whether they were born there or bought as servants.*
>
> Genesis 17:22–27 (NLT)

> *And Abraham's faith did not weaken, even though he knew that he was too old to be a father at the age of one hundred and that Sarah, his wife, had never been able to have children. Abraham never wavered in believing God's promise. In fact, his faith grew stronger, and in this he brought glory to God. He was absolutely convinced that God was able to do*

> *anything he promised. And because of Abraham's faith, God declared him to be righteous.*
>
> Romans 4:19–22 (NLT)

I believe at some point Sarah still needed some reassuring. Instead, when Sarah offered, Hagar to bare them a son, Abraham yielded to the words of Sarah and to his flesh, rather than to the word of God. The Lord himself had spoken to Abraham concerning their son several times. But Sarah was still in disbelief and eager for a child. And like Sarah, we often become doubtful or impatient, because of our great longing to have something or someone. So we try and do it ourselves in our own time and way.

Now the appointed time had arrived for Sarah to become a mother. One more time the Lord comes to speak with Abraham, in chapter eighteen, just a year before Isaac was to be born. Only this time he comes in person as the angel of the Lord, escorted by two of his angels. He came to reaffirm his promise of a son through the womb of Sarah. This is the visit where Sarah laughs at what the Lord said concerning her and Abraham having a son. I guess by this time the Lord thought within himself, *Well since you two think this is so funny, name him Isaac*, meaning *laughter*. That'll teach yah! It's not nice to laugh at God. He gets the last laugh. The Lord has such a wonderful sense of humor.

No, the Lord knew this day would come and that it would bring them much joy and laughter. He loves to bless us and see us happy and full of joy. Yes, it was the Lord's will for Isaac to be born from the beginning of creation. He also knew what Abraham and Sarah would do and what he would name their son too.

All this took place when the Lord was on his way to Sodom

and Gomorrah to judge the people there. Sarah laughed because she doubted the word of the Lord concerning Isaac's birth. She laughed as if it were the first time she had heard it. Surely Abraham told her when the Lord first gave him the promise. Like her, most of us would have given up. We probably would have said something like, *Who are these men? And how can one of them say, I am going to have a son? They don't know anything about me. Don't they see how old I am?* But she did not know it was the Lord, nor did she know the other men were angels. The word of God warns us to be careful how we treat people, because we never know when we are in the presence of angels.

> *Continue to love each other with true Christian love. Don't forget to show hospitality to strangers, for some who have done this have entertained angels without realizing it!*
> Hebrews 13:1–2 (NLT)

When Sarah laughed at the Lord's words, it didn't anger him, but he seemed displeased. I love how the Lord handled it. He addressed Abraham instead of Sarah, as to why she laughed, as if Abraham had not assured her of his promise, regardless of how long it would take.

> *The Lord appeared again to Abraham while he was camped near the oak grove belonging to Mamre. One day about noon, as Abraham was sitting at the entrance to his tent, he suddenly noticed three men standing nearby. He got up and ran to meet them, welcoming them by bowing low to the ground. "My lord," he said, "if it pleases you, stop here for a while. Rest in the shade of this tree while my servants get some water to wash your feet. Let me prepare some food to refresh you. Please stay awhile before continuing on your journey." "All right," they said. "Do as you have said." "Where*

> *is Sarah, your wife?" they asked him. "In the tent," Abraham replied. Then one of them said, "About this time next year I will return, and your wife Sarah will have a son." Now Sarah was listening to this conversation from the tent nearby. And since Abraham and Sarah were both very old, and Sarah was long past the age of having children, she laughed silently to herself. "How could a worn-out woman like me have a baby?" she thought. "And when my master—my husband—is also so old?" Then the Lord said to Abraham, "Why did Sarah laugh? Why did she say, 'Can an old woman like me have a baby?' Is anything too hard for the Lord?*
>
> *About a year from now, just as I told you, I will return, and Sarah will have a son." Sarah was afraid, so she denied that she had laughed. But he said, "That is not true. You did laugh."*
>
> Genesis 18:1–15 (NLT)

Now, Sarah acted as if she had never heard she was going to have a son. I guess she never did believe it. Can you imagine the look on Sarah's face when the Lord asked her why she laughed? She was probably frightened and wondering how could he have known she had laughed within herself.

The Lord addressed Abraham because he had given his word to him over and over again and because Abraham (and not Sarah) had the authority over his house and everything under his lordship. Maybe this was why Sarah blamed Abraham for taking Hagar as she had suggested? I believe Sarah felt that Abraham had failed to cover and protect her in this area, trusting that he would make the right decision concerning her and their future, since he was the one who heard from God. Sarah honored and reverenced Abraham. She even called him lord.

> *For in this manner, in former times, the holy women who trusted in God also adorned themselves, being submissive*

> *to their own husbands, as Sarah obeyed Abraham, calling him lord, whose daughters you are if you do good and are not afraid with any terror.*
> 2 Peter 5–6 (NKJV)

Here, he missed looking out for her best interests at that particular time. She blamed Abraham later for Hagar's situation. She felt wronged and deprived of her rights, and then she told him the Lord will judge.

> *Then Sarai said to Abram, "May (the responsibility for) my wrong and deprivation of rights be upon you. I gave my maid into your bosom and when she saw she was with child, I was contemptible and despised in her eyes. May the Lord be judge between you and me.*
> Genesis 16:5 (AMP)

I believe she felt he could have intervened by not allowing it to be so, even though she was in distress for a child. Remember, God had spoken to Abraham numerous times concerning all of his promises. Perhaps Abraham, like some of us do, had grown weary and begun to doubt, and therefore, he listened to the word of Sarah rather than the word of God, just like Adam when he missed it, yielding to the word of his wife, Eve, over the word of God. (And just look at the mess that decision made.)

Or maybe, like a typical man, Abraham was trying to please his wife, whom he loved so much, and he too wanted an heir. Or maybe he was just being a human? It appeared that Abraham didn't care much for Hagar. When Sarah got angry with her, Abraham told Sarah to do whatever she wanted with Hagar, since she was her maidservant. This was true, but she was also carrying his child. Not only did he yield to the words of Sarah, he put his trust in his flesh.

I have often wondered why the Lord used circumcision as a sign of his covenant promise to Abraham. I know this has spiritual implications, where the Word of God speaks of circumcision of the heart. Now, I believe God commanded circumcision of the flesh in the natural as a reminder of what happened when Abraham put his faith in his flesh by sleeping with Hagar. I believe it was meant to be a natural reminder for man, never to put their trust in their flesh. It sure makes sense.

> *This is My covenant which you shall keep, between Me and you and your descendants after you: Every male child among you shall be circumcised; and you shall be circumcised in the flesh of your foreskins, and it shall be a sign of the covenant between Me and you.*
> Genesis 17:10–11 (NKJV)

> *For we are the circumcision, who worship God in the Spirit, rejoice in Christ Jesus, and have no confidence in the flesh,*
> Philippians 3:3 (NKJV)

We women love to talk and give our input. We can't help it. It's a part of our makeup as women. Not only that, but we feel a need to share what is on our hearts. When the Lord said "study to be quiet," I do believe he was talking to mostly women. It is something we really do have to study to do.

> *And that ye study to be quiet, and to do your own business, and to work with your own hands, as we commanded you;*
> 1 Thessalonians 4:11 (KJV)

To all the men folks out there, when the Lord God has given you a word for your family and you know it without a doubt, don't pay any attention to us. No! No! No! Just kidding! You should listen to your wife because God speaks to her too. Couples should always communicate, and the wife should share in the decision-making. However, the final decision belongs to the head. And *when you know that you know that you know that you know*, the Lord has spoken to you and given you a word beyond the shadow of doubt, please, "Hear ye him!" Follow the voice of the Lord. Or you will make a big mess of things like Adam and Abraham. If your decision is on behalf of your own selfish ambitions, that isn't God! And that would make a big mess of things for sure.

Love obeys the word of God, and love is always looking for what is best for its family and others.

> *Those who obey my commandments are the ones who love me.*
> John 14:21a (NLT)

> *For jealousy and selfishness are not God's kind of wisdom. Such things are earthly, unspiritual, and motivated by the devil. For wherever there is jealousy and selfish ambition, there you will find disorder and every kind of evil.*
> James 3:15–16 (NLT)

For thirteen long years Abraham received not a word from the Lord. Then the Lord paid Abraham another visit. He came because it was time for him to keep his word to Abraham, despite what had been done before. Even though we fail sometimes to be faithful, the Lord still remains faithful to his word and to us. What love and grace!

> *If we are unfaithful, he remains faithful, for he cannot deny himself.*
> 2 Timothy 2:13 (NLT)

I'm sure Abraham would not have made that decision to birth a child with Hagar had he known the confusion and strife it would caused. Hagar despised Sarah. Sarah felt she had been wronged and couldn't stand Hagar and Ishmael's behavior. This conflict of interest between these women, have been passed down, through each of their sons, Isaac and Ishmael, and these descendants are still at odds with each other in the Middle East to this very day.

If you do a thorough study of these two sons, Isaac was the type who did not like confrontation. He would avoid it in whatever way he could. Isaac (*laughter*) was a peaceful man. He was not one to stir up trouble. Isaac went to live in the land of Gerar, just as the Lord had told him. But the men of the land harassed him. However, he would not retaliate. He wanted to keep peace with them. Three times his men dug wells, and the men of the city kept taking them from him. He got into a few arguments, but Isaac was not the fighting and bullying type. He would just move on and dig another well. Finally, they left him alone.

> *The Lord appeared to him there and said, "Do not go to Egypt. Do as I say, and stay here in this land. If you do, I will be with you and bless you. I will give all this land to you and your descendants, just as I solemnly promised Abraham, your father. I will do this because Abraham listened to me and obeyed all my requirements, commands, regulations, and laws."*
>
> *So Isaac moved to the Gerar Valley and lived there instead. He reopened the wells his father had dug, which the Philistines had filled in after Abraham's death. Isaac renamed them, using the names Abraham had given them. His shepherds also dug in the Gerar Valley and found a gushing spring. But then the local shepherds came and claimed the spring. "This is our water," they said, and they argued over it*

> *with Isaac's herdsmen. So Isaac named the well "Argument," because they had argued about it with him. Isaac's men then dug another well, but again there was a fight over it. So Isaac named it "Opposition." Abandoning that one, he dug another well, and the local people finally left him alone. So Isaac called it "Room Enough," for he said, "At last the Lord has made room for us, and we will be able to thrive."*
> Genesis 26:1–5, 17–22 (NLT)

Today the descendants of Isaac *(laughter)* are peaceful people. And they too are being pushed around. They too, like Isaac, try to avoid confrontation at all cost. But a day is coming when God will not allow Israel to be pushed around any longer or taken from her land.

> *This is what the Lord, the God of Israel, says: Write down for the record everything I have said to you, Jeremiah. For the time is coming when I will restore the fortunes of my people of Israel and Judah. I will bring them home to this land that I gave to their ancestors, and they will possess it and live here again. I, the Lord, have spoken!"*
> Jeremiah 30:2–3 (NLT)

Now, Ishmael (*God hears*) was a totally different story. It was Ishmael who picked on Isaac when he was a young boy. And his descendants still pick on the descendants of Isaac (Israel) today. This spirit of animosity still exists in these descendants because of Hagar's disposition toward Isaac's mother and because he was not the promised child of Abraham.

I tell you, this thing goes a lot deeper than the surface. It's not just a land battle; it's a spiritual battle as well. It's a battle against good and evil, between Satan, the fallen angel, and Jesus, the risen Savior! God promised to send a Redeemer, a Savior, the Messiah, through Isaac, the child of promise. Ishmael despised his brother like Hagar despised Sarah.

Of Ishmael's lineage came twelve sons. They were the twelve princes God told Hagar her son would have. They ran over all their brothers. Through these princes the Arabic nations were formed. Ishmael died at the age of 137. His descendants live in an area that runs from Havilah to Shur, which borders on Egypt, all the way to Assyria. This area is modern day Iraq today.

Isaac had two sons, Esau and Jacob. Jacob was the youngest son, and he had twelve sons and one daughter. His sons make up the twelve tribes of Israel. The animosity between these two descendants could have been avoided because God told Hagar she would have more descendants than she could count too. The Lord told her he was going to make a great nation of Ishmael, so there was no need for her or her son to be at odds with their other side of the family. Nevertheless, she had an attitude, and it influenced Ishmael greatly. God told both Hagar and Abraham what he was going to do for both sons.

> Then the angel of the LORD said, "Return to your mistress and submit to her authority."
> The angel added, "I will give you more descendants than you can count." And the angel also said, "You are now pregnant and will give birth to a son. You are to name him Ishmael, for the LORD has heard about your misery. This son of yours will be a wild one—free and untamed as a wild donkey! He will be against everyone, and everyone will be against him. Yes, he will live at odds with the rest of his brothers."
> Genesis 16:9–12 (NLT)

> And Abraham said to God, "Yes, may Ishmael enjoy your special blessing!" But God replied, "Sarah, your wife, will bear you a son. You will name him Isaac, and I will confirm

> *my everlasting covenant with him and his descendants. As for Ishmael, I will bless him also, just as you have asked. I will cause him to multiply and become a great nation. Twelve princes will be among his descendants. But my covenant is with Isaac, who will be born to you and Sarah about this time next year."*
>
> Genesis 17:18–21 (NLT)

Back in Genesis chapter seventeen, the Lord changed Abram's name, meaning *"exalted father"* to Abraham, meaning *"father of many nations."* His wife's name was Sarai, meaning *"contentious,"* and her name was changed to Sarah, meaning *"princess."* The changing of their names prophetically spoke of their destiny. That is how God operates. He first determines the end of a thing or event, and then he let it run its course, from the beginning to the end.

Hagar's name means *"Stranger."* It also means *"flight"* and that's exactly what happened to her. She and her son were put to flight by way of the desert because of Sarah. No! It was because God had another plan for her. Was her name and all that she encountered just a coincidence? Not at all! God reveals destinies through a promise and even by a name and he always carries it to full completion. "Destiny Hidden In A Name" is one of the major subjects I have covered in great detail, in one of my upcoming books, so please be on the lookout for them.

Abraham also had six other sons by his third wife, Keturah, whom he married after Sarah's death. Abraham later sent them to the east to live. I point this out because so many others have not. And I am sure it is no big secret. If so, the Lord would not have revealed it to us.

> *Now Abraham married again. Keturah was his new wife, and she bore him Zimran, Jokshan, Medan, Midian, Ishbak,*

> *and Shuah. Jokshan's two sons were Sheba and Dedan. Dedan's descendants were the Asshurites, Letushites, and Leummites. Midian's sons were Ephah, Epher, Hanoch, Abida, and Eldaah. These were all descendants of Abraham through Keturah. Abraham left everything he owned to his son Isaac. But before he died, he gave gifts to the sons of his concubines and sent them off to the east, away from Isaac.*
> Genesis 25:1–6 (NLT)

These sons were sent away, just like Ishmael. I believe all of this was a part of God's will concerning them too. The men of the east in the word of God are often called wise men. They were wise, great, and wealthy. Job was also from the east and he was wise and he was extremely wealthy. It was wise men, not kings, like many of us have been taught and proclaimed, that traveled all the way to Bethlehem, searching for the Lord Jesus when he was born. Every translation I have looked at says, "Wise men." Some referred to them as astrologers. Could it be that the wise men that found Jesus when he was a child are the descendants of the sons of Abraham whom he sent away to the east? Maybe these descendants of Abraham were sent away to the east for such a time as this. I am sure Abraham told all his sons during their times together, that one day the promise of the Messiah was sure to come and I believe these sons passed it on down to their descendants.

> *Now after Jesus was born in Bethlehem of Judea in the days of Herod the king, behold, wise men from the East came to Jerusalem, saying, "Where is He who has been born King of the Jews? For we have seen His star in the East and have come to worship Him."*
> Matthew 2:1–2 (NKJV)

Though Ishmael was sent away from Isaac, he and Isaac both buried their father Abraham together. That means though they were apart, they kept in touch. I believe Isaac also kept in touch with his other half brothers, who were the sons of Abraham's last wife, Keturah, also referred to as his concubine.

> *Abraham left everything he owned to his son Isaac. But before he died, he gave gifts to the sons of his concubines and sent them off to the east, away from Isaac. Abraham lived for 175 years, and he died at a ripe old age, joining his ancestors in death. His sons Isaac and Ishmael buried him in the cave of Machpelah, near Mamre, in the field of Ephron son of Zohar the Hittite.*
> Genesis 25:5–9 (NLT)

When God makes a promise, it is a perpetual one, and he never forgets them. And he never forgets us, no matter who our parents are or where we are from. He has a purpose for all of us.

The Lord made a promise to Abraham, and he made a promise to Hagar. And he brought it all to pass. I believe God again will one day hear the cry of Ishmael's descendants in the Middle East and set the record straight with them once and for all concerning their brothers and what land belongs to whom. The Lord promised certain land in the east to Abraham and his descendants. He also said the promise of the Messiah would come through Isaac, his son and it was so. God also made a promise to Abraham to bless Ishmael. God said that in Abraham, all the families of the earth would be blessed, that includes the descendants of Ishmael, the Arabs. In fact many of them have come to faith in Jesus Christ here in the last few years. Many of them have done it secretly, because they fear what could happen to them for becoming a Christian; Just like Nicodemus did in Jesus' day, because he fear the Jewish leaders, the same Nicodemus who helped with Jesus' burial.

> *There was a man of the Pharisees named Nicodemus, a ruler of the Jews. This man came to Jesus by night and said to Him, "Rabbi, we know that You are a teacher come from God; for no one can do these signs that You do unless God is with him."*
>
> John 3:1–2 (NKJV)

> *And Nicodemus, who at first came to Jesus by night, also came, bringing a mixture of myrrh and aloes, about a hundred pounds. 40 Then they took the body of Jesus, and bound it in strips of linen with the spices, as the custom of the Jews is to bury.*
>
> John 19:39–40 (NKJV)

God is not a God of divisions but a God of reconciliation. God reconciled Joseph and his brothers. He reconciled Jacob and Esau. Just as he through Jesus Christ reconciles us to him. There is also a day appointed by God when he will reconcile the Jews back to the one whom they rejected. It is in Jesus Christ, The Messiah, that God will reconcile those who are still lost and I believe one day he will reconcile the descendants of these two brothers who are so at odds with each other—those of them who will to be reconciled! But all who reject Jesus, will experience the wrath of God, in the end.

> *Oh, what a wonderful God we have! How great are his riches and wisdom and knowledge! How impossible it is for us to understand his decisions and his methods! For who can know what the Lord is thinking? Who knows enough to be his counselor? And who could ever give him so much that he would have to pay it back? For everything comes from him; everything exists by his power and is intended for his glory. To him be glory evermore. Amen*
>
> Romans 11:33–36 (NLT)

Knowing Your Child's Destiny Before Birth

The Lord gave me a message. He said, "I knew you before I formed you in your mother's womb. Before you were born I set you apart and appointed you as my spokesman to the world."
Jeremiah 1:4–5 (NLT)

Some parents knew their children's preplanned destiny before their children were born. Some of these parents knew their child's destiny before their children were ever conceived in the womb. I want to make sure all you wonderful mothers out there, married or single, to notice later as we begin to discuss this, how God addressed some of these women first concerning the children he was sending. He appeared to them first and told them what was going to happen and he revealed to them the child's gender and the child's purpose.

I believe God was not only honoring these women with his wonderful plan, but he was showing respect to these women, since they were the ones to carry the child in the womb and because they would have a great influence in their child's life. God is indeed a God of order and he is a gentleman who is very kind and full of compassion.

We are going to look at a few other examples of parents who knew their child's appointed destiny before birth.

The First Genocide
(Amram and Jochebed)

Amram and Jochebed were the parents of Moses. Amram means, *"Exalted people."* And God exalted them before the eyes of all nations and he will do it again. Amram was a grandson of Kohath, Abraham's descendant. Moses mother, Jochebed, means *"Yahweh's Glory."* And that's just what God did. He displayed his glory through Jochebed's son, Moses.

When Moses was born, Pharaoh charged his soldiers to kill all the male Hebrew children, from birth to the age of two, but they were ordered not to kill the baby girls. The reason Pharaoh wanted the Hebrew boys to die was because the children of Israel were multiplying in great numbers and he and his peers feared they might ally with their enemies in a time of war and flee the country.

> *Then a new king came to the throne of Egypt who knew nothing about Joseph or what he had done. He told his people, "These Israelites are becoming a threat to us because there are so many of them. We must find a way to put an end to this. If we don't and if war breaks out, they will join our enemies and fight against us. Then they will escape from the country." So the Egyptians made the Israelites their slaves and put brutal slave drivers over them, hoping to wear them down under heavy burdens. They forced them*

to build the cities of Pithom and Rameses as supply centers for the king. But the more the Egyptians oppressed them, the more quickly the Israelites multiplied! The Egyptians soon became alarmed.

Exodus 1:8–12 (NLT)

The Egyptians increased their burden even more by making them to make mortal and brick and they were made to work a lot longer than before. When that didn't work the King of Egypt ordered the Hebrew midwives to commit genocide on the male seed. They wouldn't because they feared the Almighty God and He protected and blessed them because of their reference for Him. Then Pharaoh commanded his own people, to do this horrendous and brutal act of murder on the Hebrew male child.

Then Pharaoh, the king of Egypt, gave this order to the Hebrew midwives, Shiphrah and Puah: "When you help the Hebrew women give birth, kill all the boys as soon as they are born. Allow only the baby girls to live." But because the midwives feared God, they refused to obey the king and allowed the boys to live, too. Then the king called for the midwives. "Why have you done this?" he demanded. "Why have you allowed the boys to live?" "Sir," they told him, "the Hebrew women are very strong. They have their babies so quickly that we cannot get there in time! They are not slow in giving birth like Egyptian women." So God blessed the midwives, and the Israelites continued to multiply, growing more and more powerful. And because the midwives feared God, he gave them families of their own. Then Pharaoh gave this order to all his people: "Throw all the newborn Israelite boys into the Nile River. But you may spare the baby girls."

Exodus 1:15–22 (NLT)

Moses parents saw in him something great. His mother saw how beautiful he was and she knew he was a special child. Because of her love for him and her faith in God she hid him for three months. Not able to hide him any longer, she placed him in a basket and placed him in the hand of God upon the Nile River.

> *During this time, a man and woman from the tribe of Levi got married. The woman became pregnant and gave birth to a son. She saw what a beautiful baby he was and kept him hidden for three months. But when she could no longer hide him, she got a little basket made of papyrus reeds and waterproofed it with tar and pitch. She put the baby in the basket and laid it among the reeds along the edge of the Nile River. The baby's sister then stood at a distance, watching to see what would happen to him.*
>
> Exodus 2:1–4 (NLT)

The Lord caused the little basket to flow to the house of Pharaoh's daughter. That's the sovereignty of our God. When she saw him, she knew right away that he was a Hebrew baby, and she had pity on him. Moses' little sister was watching when she took him from the river.

> *Soon after this, one of Pharaoh's daughters came down to bathe in the river, and her servant girls walked along the riverbank. When the princess saw the little basket among the reeds, she told one of her servant girls to get it for her. As the princess opened it, she found the baby boy. His helpless cries touched her heart. "He must be one of the Hebrew children," she said.*
>
> Exodus 2:5–6 (NLT)

When Moses' sister saw that Pharaoh's daughter showed compassion for him, she came to her and asked if she wanted her to go and get someone to nurse him for her, and she said, yes. So Moses' sister Miriam, meaning *"prophetess,"* went and got *"Yahweh's glory,"* who is Jochebed, their mother, and told her the good news. I can just imagine the joy Miriam expressed to her mother concerning Moses. He lives! He lives! Moses is safe. Pharaoh's daughter has taken him from the Nile River and into her bosom. "Come!" The Lord has arranged for you to nurse your own son right under Pharaoh's daughter roof.

> *Then his sister said to Pharaoh's daughter, "Shall I go and call a nurse for you from the Hebrew women, that she may nurse the child for you?" And Pharaoh's daughter said to her, "Go." So the maiden went and called the child's mother.*
> Exodus 2:7–8 (NKJV)

Pharaoh's daughter named him Moses because she said she drew him from the Nile River. So, Moses sister went and got their mother. Pharaoh's daughter claimed Moses as her own child, but his mother cared for him.

The Lord had preplanned for Pharaoh's daughter to keep and protect him until the time for him to draw out the children of Israel because the time was at hand for the Lord to fulfill his promise to Abraham. No matter what kind of plans a man makes, when it goes against the plan of God, it will not succeed. Only his plan will stand, and he will use those who buck it to fulfill it.

> *You can make many plans, but the LORD's purpose will prevail.*
> Proverbs 19:21 (NLT)

The hand of God was on Pharaoh's daughter. She didn't have a heart like her father. She saw a life, her motherly instincts kicked in, and she kept him alive. Her father saw fear and the possibility of losing his kingdom, because the Hebrews had increased in numbers mightily. What he feared eventually came to pass, because he was wicked, he brutally enslaved the people of God and because he had no knowledge of the True and Living God. The Lord used Pharaoh's daughter to preserve Moses' life and paid his mother to nurse him, while he grew, right under Pharaoh's nose.

> *Then Pharaoh's daughter said to her, "Take this child away and nurse him for me, and I will give you your wages." So the woman took the child and nursed him. And the child grew, and she brought him to Pharaoh's daughter, and he became her son. So she called his name Moses, saying, "Because I drew him out of the water."*
> Exodus 2:9–10 (NKJV)

Moses' mother knew when he was born that the Lord had a special plan for his life. She knew in her heart that he would live and fulfill God's will. Not only did she nurse him, I believe she was like a nanny to him, this allowed her to teach him all about the God of Abraham, Isaac, and Jacob and to fear God rather than embrace the life of the Egyptians. When Moses grew up, he rejected the pleasures of Egypt and pursued the true and living God—the God of Abraham, Isaac, and Jacob/Israel. The Lord sent Moses into the earth to deliver the Children of Israel out of bitter bondage, just as he promised Abraham he would do after a period of 400 years.

The Egyptian meaning for Moses is *"Son"* the Hebrew suggested meaning is *"Deliver"* and *"Drawn out."* The Lord fulfilled his purpose through Moses by using him to deliver and draw out Abraham's descendants from slavery in Egypt, into the land of promise.

> *Then the LORD told Abram, "You can be sure that your descendants will be strangers in a foreign land, and they will be oppressed as slaves for four hundred years. But I will punish the nation that enslaves them, and in the end they will come away with great wealth. (But you will die in peace, at a ripe old age.) After four generations your descendants will return here to this land, when the sin of the Amorites has run its course."*
> Genesis 15:13–16 (NLT)

> *The people of Israel had lived in Egypt for 430 years. In fact, it was on the last day of the 430 th year that all the LORD's forces left the land. This night had been reserved by the LORD to bring his people out from the land of Egypt, so this same night now belongs to him. It must be celebrated every year, from generation to generation, to remember the LORD's deliverance.*
> Exodus 12:40–42 (NLT)

The Lord is not forgetful or unfaithful to keep his word like people. When he says he will do something it is as good as done, no matter how long it may take. He forgets no one and he forgets nothing, except the sins of a sincerely repented person.

> *"I, even I, am He who blots out your transgressions for My own sake; And I will not remember your sins. Put Me in remembrance; Let us contend together; State your case, that you may be acquitted.*
> Isaiah 43:25–26 (NKJV)

Nothing can describe the horror those Hebrew mothers and their families went through. Seeing their children stripped from their arms and murdered like that. It had to have been far worse than we could ever think. Imagine how God must have felt to look down from heaven and see a river full of slaughtered Hebrew babies.

Some of you may be thinking, *Why didn't God do something?* I can't give you one sure answer. But I do know all those children are with him. And they are better off with the Lord than to suffer under the hand of a wicked Pharaoh. Sometimes the Lord allows things to happen because a time has been set for all things. The word of God states that an event or a nation or even a person has a course in life and it has to run its course. Often after it has run its course you see God pouring out his blessings or judgments according to whatever was done. No matter how long it may seem, the Lord is a God of justice, and he will pay everyone according to his or her deeds, whether good or evil.

The things the Lord declared concerning Pharaoh came to past. All the firstborn of the Egyptians died, including Pharaoh's son. The Lord stripped him of his power, wealth, and human resources. He took the children of Israel from his brutal slavery. When they were finally gone, Pharaoh became very angry and sent his army after them. The Lord looked down from heaven, saw Pharaoh wicked actions and overthrew his plans, drowning his whole army in the Red Sea. All male army! He reaped just what he had sown.

> *So the children of Israel went into the midst of the sea on the dry ground, and the waters were a wall to them on their right hand and on their left. And the Egyptians pursued and went after them into the midst of the sea, all Pharaoh's horses, his chariots, and his horsemen. Now it came to pass, in the morning watch, that the* LORD *looked down upon the army of the Egyptians through the pillar of fire and cloud,*

> *and He troubled the army of the Egyptians. And He took off their chariot wheels, so that they drove them with difficulty; and the Egyptians said, "Let us flee from the face of Israel, for the* LORD *fights for them against the Egyptians." Then the* LORD *said to Moses, "Stretch out your hand over the sea, that the waters may come back upon the Egyptians, on their chariots, and on their horsemen." And Moses stretched out his hand over the sea; and when the morning appeared, the sea returned to its full depth, while the Egyptians were fleeing into it. So the* LORD *overthrew the Egyptians in the midst of the sea. Then the waters returned and covered the chariots, the horsemen, and all the army of Pharaoh that came into the sea after them. Not so much as one of them remained.*
> Exodus 14:22–28 (NKJV)

Yes, the tides were turned. God will not be mocked! What is sown, that is what will be reaped. No nation will get away with anything. From the millions of aborted babies in the U.S. to genocide in Sudan, God has a time appointed for judging everything and everyone.

Oh, by the way, the Sudanese are descendants of Abraham. These descendants were among the children of Israel when Moses brought them out of Egypt. At that time, they were referred to as the Nubians. By the wisdom of God, Cecil B. DeMille included a very short scene of this tribe of people in his masterpiece "The Ten Commandments." When the children of Israel had gathered together to leave Egypt, this beautiful black tribe of Nubians came marching through the crowds beating their drums. At this point, a boy playing the role of a little Hebrew son pointed at them and said to his grandfather, "Look grandfather, Nubians!" Now that was no coincidence. Nor was it a coincidence that the Holy Spirit reminded me of this scene in the movie during the time the media was carrying coverage about the genocide in Sudan and other parts of Africa. It was also during the time I was doing some revision on this chapter of my book.

Studies show that the Nubians and the Sudanese people are one nation. And just as God judged those that oppressed and killed the Hebrews, he will judge those that have oppressed and killed the Sudanese. He will also judge those who have enslaved and killed his people in other nations around the world and for the ones they are oppressing today.

God says:

> *"At the time I have planned, I will bring justice against the wicked"*
>
> Psalm 75:2 (NLT)

Another Appointed Womb (Hannah)

Hannah, meaning *"grace,"* was one of Elkanah's wives. His other wife, Peninnah, teased Hannah very badly for years. Peninnah caused Hannah much grief because she didn't have any children. This grieved Hannah very much to the point she would cry and not eat. One day she went to the temple in Shiloh and poured out her heart to God for a son. She vowed to the Lord that if he would give her a son, she would give him back to him to serve him. Sure enough, at the appointed time, the Lord graciously answered her prayer and gave her a son. She named him Samuel meaning, *"The Lord hears."*

> *Then they rose early in the morning and worshiped before the LORD, and returned and came to their house at Ramah. And Elkanah knew Hannah his wife, and the LORD remembered her. So it came to pass in the process of time that Hannah*

> *conceived and bore a son, and called his name Samuel, saying, "Because I have asked for him from the LORD."*
> 1 Samuel 1:19–20 (NKJV)

The Lord preserved Hannah's womb until the appointed time. He knew he would need a prophet to speak to the kings of the children of Israel because they were asking that a king rule over them like all the other nations. So, the Lord appointed a prophet to speak to the kings of Israel and the leaders of the surrounding nations. He still does today.

After weaning Samuel, she kept her word and took him to the temple with another offering for the Lord. Each year she went to visit her son Samuel and took him a garment which she made. Yes, his mother was a seamstress, too. Samuel grew up in the temple of God at Shiloh and served the Lord God as a prophet all the days of his life.

> *Now Samuel, though only a boy, was the LORD's helper. He wore a linen tunic just like that of a priest. Each year his mother made a small coat for him and brought it to him when she came with her husband for the sacrifice.*
> 1 Samuel 2:18–19 (NLT)

The Lord was pleased with Hannah's prayer and He answered her. Hannah kept her, vow, which she made to the Lord and He honors her again by giving her 5 more children.

> *And the LORD gave Hannah three sons and two daughters. Meanwhile, Samuel grew up in the presence of the LORD.*
> 1 Samuel 2:21 (NLT)

Samuel anointed Israel's first king, a young man name Saul, and he anointed David as their next king when King Saul rebelled against the Lord. He spoke for the Lord and was a prophet to the children of Israel and Kings of Israel until the day he died. Samuel even prophesied King Saul's final fate from the grave. Samuel lived a long full life and was a great prophet of God. You can read the entire passages about his life as the prophet of the Lord in the Old Testament, I and II Samuel.

> *So Samuel grew, and the LORD was with him and let none of his words fall to the ground. And all Israel from Dan to Beersheba knew that Samuel had been established as a prophet of the LORD.*
>
> 1 Samuel 3:19–21 (NKJV)

> *As they were going down to the outskirts of the city, Samuel said to Saul, "Tell the servant to go on ahead of us." And he went on. "But you stand here awhile, that I may announce to you the word of God."*
>
> I Samuel 9:27 (NKJV)

God is a good God. I want to encourage all the couples believing the Lord for a child, do not give up. Continue to have faith in God and he will bring it to pass, at its appointed time. You may one day come home from worshipping the Lord as Elkanah and Hannah did and you too may experience the same blessing. The Lord did it for them. He did it for Zacharias and Elizabeth, this next couple, who was very old in age and he has done it for so many others. Every child the Lord sends here, he has a purpose and an appointed time for their arrival. The Lord loves children and he wants us to have them, but he doesn't just send them so a woman can have a baby. He wants to fulfill a need in the earth for our benefit and for his glory. That is why it is important to seek the Lord for your child or children's purpose, so that you may successfully help them to prepare and fulfill it.

Birth of the Lord's Best Man
(Zacharias and Elizabeth)

Zacharias and Elizabeth were the parents of John the Baptist. Zacharias was a Levite, and he served as a priest unto the Lord among the children of Israel. For years, they prayed to the Lord for a child. Like Abraham and Sarah, the Lord God answered their prayers in their old age.

The angel of the Lord visited Zacharias, meaning *"Yahweh"* while he was serving in the temple and told him that he and his wife, Elizabeth, meaning *"My God is an oath"* were going to have a child. The angel of the Lord also told him the child's gender and the child's purpose. He told him the child would be a son and to name him John. The angel also told Zacharias his son should not drink wine or hard liquor. Then he told him his son's calling.

All this was declared before the child was conceived in the womb of his wife, Elizabeth. Please notice the New Living Bible translated Zacharias' name as Zechariah.

> *Zechariah was in the sanctuary when an angel of the Lord appeared, standing to the right of the incense altar. Zechariah was overwhelmed with fear. But the angel said, "Don't be afraid, Zechariah! For God has heard your prayer, and your wife, Elizabeth, will bear you a son! And you are to name him John. You will have great joy and gladness, and many will rejoice with you at his birth, for he will be great in the eyes of the Lord. He must never touch wine or hard liquor, and he will be filled with the Holy Spirit, even before his birth. And he will persuade many Israelites to turn to the Lord their God. He will be a man with the spirit and power of Elijah, the prophet of old. He will precede the coming of the Lord, preparing the people for his arrival. He will turn the hearts of the fathers to their children, and he will change disobedient minds to accept godly wisdom."*
>
> Luke 1:11–17 (NLT)

Being so long coming to pass and they were now very old in age; Zacharias didn't believe what the angel said concerning the child. Because of that, the angel told Zacharias, he wouldn't speak again until the child was born.

> *And the angel answered and said to him, "I am Gabriel, who stands in the presence of God, and was sent to speak to you and bring you these glad tidings. But behold, you will be mute and not able to speak until the day these things take place, because you did not believe my words which will be fulfilled in their own time." And the people waited for Zacharias, and marveled that he lingered so long in the temple. But when he came out, he could not speak to them; and they perceived that he had seen a vision in the temple, for he beckoned to them and remained speechless.*
>
> Luke 1:19–22 (NKJV)

Zacharias also means, "*Yah remembered*" and Elisabeth means, "*My God has sworn an oath.*" John means, "*Yahweh has been gracious.*" The Lord keeps his promises to answer our prayer. So, never give up! He will answer at the appointed time.

> *Now Elizabeth's full time came for her to be delivered, and she brought forth a son. When her neighbors and relatives heard how the Lord had shown great mercy to her, they rejoiced with her. So it was, on the eighth day, that they came to circumcise the child; and they would have called him by the name of his father, Zacharias. His mother answered and said, "No; he shall be called John." But they said to her, "There is no one among your relatives who is called by this name." So they made signs to his father—what he would have him called. And he asked for a writing tablet, and wrote, saying, "His name is John." So they all marveled. Immediately his mouth was opened and his tongue loosed, and he spoke, praising God. Then fear came on all who dwelt around them; and all*

these sayings were discussed throughout all the hill country of Judea. And all those who heard them kept them in their hearts, saying, "What kind of child will this be?" And the hand of the Lord was with him.
                                    Luke 1:57–66 (NKJV)

John the Baptist's ministry ended in his thirties like Jesus. They were both cousins, and John was about six months older than Jesus. He lived and did just as the angel Gabriel declared. He preached the coming of the Messiah and baptized many who repented. John confronted King Herod many times about his adulterous behavior, because had married his brother's wife. Not only had he sinned by marrying his brother's wife, he also lusted after his wife's daughter. He loved to see her dance. John was put in prison and later beheaded by King Herod. It happened during King Herod's birthday celebration. He made an oath to give Herodias's daughter whatever she wanted if she would dance for him. She agreed, and after she danced for him, she asked her mother what should she ask of him? Her mother said, tell him you want John the Baptist's head on a platter.

For Herod had laid hold of John and bound him, and put him in prison for the sake of Herodias, his brother Philip's wife. Because John had said to him, "It is not lawful for you to have her." And although he wanted to put him to death, he feared the multitude, because they counted him as a prophet. But when Herod's birthday was celebrated, the daughter of Herodias danced before them and pleased Herod. Therefore he promised with an oath to give her whatever she might ask. So she, having been prompted by her mother, said, "Give me John the Baptist's head here on a platter." And the king was sorry; nevertheless, because of the oaths and because of those who sat with him, he commanded it to be given to her. So he sent and had John beheaded in prison. And his head was

brought on a platter and given to the girl, and she brought it to her mother. Then his disciples came and took away the body and buried it, and went and told Jesus.
Matthew 14:3–12 (NKJV)

John the Baptist knew his purpose before his parents, Zechariah and Elizabeth, could tell him. He leaped for joy in his mother's womb at the sound of Mary's voice. Even though John the Baptist died a horrible death, he fulfilled his purpose. Jesus himself said, "John the Baptist was the greatest prophet that ever lived," (Luke 7:28).

Many men and women, young and old were martyred because of their belief and confession in Jesus—men and women like Stephen, a disciple of Jesus who was stoned to death by a religious group of men from Cyrene, Alexandria, and those from Cilicia and Asia. They were all gathered together at the place called the Synagogue of the Freedmen. King Herod beheaded James, one of the apostles of Jesus. The apostle Peter was later crucified for preaching about Jesus, the Son of God. Men like John Frith and Andrew Hewet were burned to death. And thousands of others even up to our present day are still being persecuted for their faith in Jesus.

On April 20, 1999, Rachel Scott and Cassie Barnard was gun down by a fellow student in the Columbine School killings. When one of the shooters asked if she believed in God and she said, "Yes!" After her death, there were several interviews of her family and friends talking about her life. They talked about her growing faith in the Lord and that she would write in her journal things the Lord would reveal to her concerning her life. They stated, she said she knew her purpose and she was ready. After her death, thousands of young people made a confession of faith in Jesus, the Son of God.

Sometimes life does not always end in what we call a happy ending. But a happy ending is really a life that has fulfilled its purpose, no matter what the calling.

The Birth of the Bridegroom (Joseph and the Virgin Mary)

Gabriel the archangel of the Lord, the same one who appeared to Zacharias in the temple appeared to a young virgin name Mary. He revealed to her first that she was going to have a son. He told her what to name him and what his purpose was. Mary did not doubt the words of the angel, unlike Zacharias. Although she had been espoused to Joseph, she was still a virgin. The espousal period lasted one year, and during this time, there was no sexual contact. So Mary asked the angel Gabriel, how could it be, knowing she was not married, nor had she been sexually intimate.

The angel told her that she would conceive a child when the power of the Holy Spirit overshadowed her. He told her who the child was, the child's purpose and agenda.

> *Now in the sixth month the angel Gabriel was sent by God to a city of Galilee named Nazareth, to a virgin betrothed to a man whose name was Joseph, of the house of David. The virgin's name was Mary. And having come in, the angel said to her, "Rejoice, highly favored one, the Lord is with you; blessed are you among women!" But when she saw him, she was troubled at his saying, and considered what manner of greeting this was. Then the angel said to her, "Do not be afraid, Mary, for you have found favor with God. And behold, you will conceive in your womb and bring forth a Son, and shall call His name JESUS. He will be great, and will be called the Son of the Highest; and the Lord God will give Him the throne of His father David. And He will reign over the house of Jacob forever, and of His kingdom there will be no end."*

> *Then Mary said to the angel, "How can this be, since I do not know a man?" And the angel answered and said to her, "The Holy Spirit will come upon you, and the power of the Highest will overshadow you; therefore, also, that Holy One who is to be born will be called the Son of God.*
>
> Luke 1: 26–35 (NKJV)

When Joseph learned she was pregnant, he knew he was not the father and he was planning to call off the engagement. According to the laws of God, given to them through the hand of Moses, if a woman or a man was found unfaithful, the people were to stone them to death. However, Joseph was a just man, and he loved Mary. He did not want her to be put to shame, nor did he want her to die. Joseph was very grieved and disturbed over this, and he struggled in his decision as to what he should do. The weariness tired him out among other things and he fell off to sleep. Then the angel of the Lord appeared to him in a dream and confirmed all that Mary had told him. In the same details, he described what had happened to her, who the child "is," and his purpose and agenda. The Angel encouraged Joseph and told him not to be afraid to take Mary as his wife; that the child she had conceived was of the Holy Spirit. Joseph believed him and obeyed. He married Mary, and when the baby was born, they named him Jesus, just as they were told, and they raised Jesus just as our heavenly Father God had preplanned.

> *Now the birth of Jesus Christ was as follows: After His mother Mary was betrothed to Joseph, before they came together, she was found with child of the Holy Spirit. Then Joseph her husband, being a just man, and not wanting to make her a public example, was minded to put her away secretly. But while he thought about these things, behold, an angel of the Lord appeared to him in a dream, saying,*

"Joseph, son of David, do not be afraid to take to you Mary your wife, for that which is conceived in her is of the Holy Spirit. And she will bring forth a Son, and you shall call His name JESUS, for He will save His people from their sins." So all this was done that it might be fulfilled which was spoken by the Lord through the prophet, saying: "Behold, the virgin shall be with child, and bear a Son, and they shall call His name Immanuel," which is translated, "God with us." Then Joseph, being aroused from sleep, did as the angel of the Lord commanded him and took to him his wife, and did not know her till she had brought forth her firstborn Son. And he called His name JESUS.
Matthew 1:18–25 (NKJV)

Jesus fulfilled his purpose in the earth, and he has a final purpose that is yet to come. He will judge those who have received him as the only begotten son of God, Lord and Savior, at the Judgment seat of Christ. And he will judge those who rejected him, at the Great White Throne Judgement. Jesus is appointed to return to earth again with the Saints of God to set up his eternal kingdom on earth. Every government and people will be subject to his authority. He will rule and reign in the earth over all nations as Lord of lords and Kings of kings forever.

Therefore the Lord Himself will give you a sign: Behold, the virgin shall conceive and bear a Son, and shall call His name Immanuel. Curds and honey He shall eat, that He may know to refuse the evil and choose the good. For before the Child shall know to refuse the evil and choose the good, the land that you dread will be forsaken by both her kings.
Isaiah 7:14–16 (NKJV)

For a child is born to us, a son is given to us. And the government will rest on his shoulders. These will be his royal titles: Wonderful, Counselor, Mighty God, Everlasting Father,

Prince of Peace. His ever expanding, peaceful government will never end. He will rule forever with fairness and justice from the throne of his ancestor David. The passionate commitment of the LORD *Almighty will guarantee this!*
Isaiah 9:6–7 (NLT)

Now I saw heaven opened, and behold, a white horse. And He who sat on him was called Faithful and True, and in righteousness He judges and makes war. His eyes were like a flame of fire, and on His head were many crowns. He had a name written that no one knew except Himself. He was clothed with a robe dipped in blood, and His name is called The Word of God. And the armies in heaven, clothed in fine linen, white and clean, followed Him on white horses. Now out of His mouth goes a sharp sword, that with it He should strike the nations. And He Himself will rule them with a rod of iron. He Himself treads the winepress of the fierceness and wrath of Almighty God. And He has on His robe and on His thigh a name written: KING OF KINGS AND LORD OF LORDS.
Revelation 19:11–16 (NKJV)

In one of my upcoming books titled, "The Last Subpoena" I've shared more extensively on the purpose and life of the Lord Jesus Christ and our eternal destiny. I hope you will continue to look for these next books and be tremendously blessed by them.

Here Comes The Judge
(Manoah and His Barren Wife)

Throughout the entire book of Judges, the children of Israel would forsake God and worship the gods of the nations among them. Whenever they did, these nations would take them into captivity, and they would be oppressed for years. But every time this happened, they would cry out to the Lord and the Lord would raise up a person to deliver them. The Lord again, foreseeing their oppression, appointed a judge, to bring his judgment on their enemies, who at this time was the nation of the Philistines.

Let's look in more detail at the life of this child. His name was Samson and as each of us, he had an appointed destiny. His purpose was also given to his parents before he was conceived in the womb of his mother. The Lord appeared to the wife of Manoah first, concerning the birth of their son. Her name was not mentioned. She's only addressed as the wife of Manaoh.

The angel of the Lord appeared to her as she was working in the fields. He told her that although she was barren, she was going to have a son. She was instructed not to drink wine or strong drink and to not eat any thing that was unclean. He told her to never cut his hair because he would be a Nazarite unto God from the womb. He told her God was sending him to deliver the children of Israel from the Philistines.

She went and repeated all the instructions the angel had given her to Monoah her husband. He asked the Lord to send the angel back to them and give them more instructions. The Lord answered him, and the angel returned and again instructed both of them that they were to raise Samson from the womb as a Nazarite unto God.

A Nazarite was never to cut his hair, drink wine or strong drink, nor eat, or even touch anything that was unclean. The Hebrew terms for Nazarite means consecration, devotion, and separation—a person who is set apart for God's service. The word Nazarite also means "Saint" and "Christian."

> *The angel of the LORD appeared to Manoah's wife and said, "Even though you have been unable to have children,*

you will soon become pregnant and give birth to a son. You must not drink wine or any other alcoholic drink or eat any forbidden food. You will become pregnant and give birth to a son, and his hair must never be cut. For he will be dedicated to God as a Nazirite from birth. He will rescue Israel from the Philistines."
Judges 13:3–5 (NLT)

The angel of the L<small>ORD</small> replied, "Be sure your wife follows the instructions I gave her.
Judges 13:13 (NLT)

Samson knew his life's destiny from birth. His parents raised him just as God commanded them. Even though he violated the rules of the Nazarite by touching the dead lion he killed, had an unequally yoke marriage, slept with a harlot, and had an affair with another Philistine woman (all at different times, of course), he was still a Nazarite that was devoted to God. God used him in spite of his failures and weaknesses. Samson was handed over to the Philistines at Lehi. As the Philistines were rejoicing over Samson's capture, he broke free and killed them with a donkey's jawbone. After killing them, he prayed to God for water.

As Samson arrived at Lehi, the Philistines came shouting in triumph. But the Spirit of the L<small>ORD</small> powerfully took control of Samson, and he snapped the ropes on his arms as if they were burnt strands of flax, and they fell from his wrists. Then he picked up a donkey's jawbone that was lying on the ground and killed a thousand Philistines with it. And Samson said, "With the jawbone of a donkey, I've made heaps on heaps! With the jawbone of a donkey, I've killed a thousand men!"

When he finished speaking, he threw away the jawbone; and the place was named Jawbone Hill. Now Samson was very

> *thirsty, and he cried out to the LORD, "You have accomplished this great victory by the strength of your servant. Must I now die of thirst and fall into the hands of these pagan people?" So God caused water to gush out of a hollow in the ground at Lehi, and Samson was revived as he drank. Then he named that place "The Spring of the One Who Cried Out," and it is still in Lehi to this day.*
>
> Judges 15:14–19 (NLT)

I like to mention more about the three Philistine women. The Philistines were considered unclean people who worshipped false gods and were enemies of the children of Israel. Samson's first wife was a woman of Timnah. The Philistines killed her shortly after his marriage to her. Most people do not realize this, but his marriage to her was a part of God's plan to judge the Philistines.

> *One day when Samson was in Timnah, he noticed a certain woman. When he returned home, he told his father and mother, "I want to marry a young Philistine woman I saw in Timnah. His father and mother objected strenuously, "Isn't there a woman in our tribe or among all the Israelites you could marry? Why must you go to the pagan Philistines to find a wife?" But Samson told his father, "Get her for me. She is the one I want." His father and mother didn't realize that the Lord was at work in this, creating an opportunity to disrupt the Philistines, who ruled over Israel at that time.*
>
> Judges 14:1–4 (NLT)

At the reception, Samson had given the men there a riddle to solve. If they did, he was going to reward them greatly. The Philistines threatened his wife for the answer. She nagged Samson for the answer to his riddle. Finally, he gave it to her, and she gave the answer to them.

> *On the fourth day they said to Samson's wife, "Get the answer to the riddle from your husband, or we will burn down your father's house with you in it. Did you invite us to this party just to make us poor?" So Samson's wife came to him in tears and said, "You don't love me; you hate me! You have given my people a riddle, but you haven't told me the answer." "I haven't even given the answer to my father or mother," he replied. "Why should I tell you?" So she cried whenever she was with him and kept it up for the rest of the celebration. At last, on the seventh day, he told her the answer because of her persistent nagging. Then she gave the answer to the young men.*
>
> Judges 14:15–17 (NLT)

Because they threatened her for the answer, it made Samson very angry, and he went out and killed thirty Philistines men, took their garments, paid what he vowed the men, and he went back to his parent's home.

> *So before sunset of the seventh day, the men of the town came to Samson with their answer: "What is sweeter than honey? What is stronger than a lion?" Samson replied, "If you hadn't plowed with my heifer, you wouldn't have found the answer to my riddle!" Then the Spirit of the LORD powerfully took control of him. He went down to the town of Ashkelon, killed thirty men, took their belongings, and gave their clothing to the men who had answered his riddle. But Samson was furious about what had happened, and he went back home to live with his father and mother. So his wife was given in marriage to the man who had been Samson's best man at the wedding.*
>
> Judges 14:19–20 (NLT)

A few days later after he cooled off, he went back to see his wife again, but her father thought he no longer wanted her, so he gave her to Samson's best man. Then he got angry again and took three hundred foxes, tied torches to their tails, and sent them into the fields of the Philistines and burned all their grain, grapevines, and olive trees. When they realized it was Samson who caused it, they went to his father-in-law and wife's home and burned them to death. This made Samson extremely angry and he went and killed more Philistines and then went away to live in a cave.

> *"Who did this?" the Philistines demanded. "Samson," was the reply, because his father-in-law from Timnah gave Samson's wife to his best man." So the Philistines went and got the woman and her father and burned them to death.*
> Judges 15:6 (NLT)

Now why would they want to go and do a thing like that? They were not just contending with Samson this time, they were contending with God. When Samson used the foxes to set fire to their fields, after finding out his father-in-law gave away his wife, the Word of God says, the Spirit of the Lord came upon him.

The second Philistine woman Samson got involved with was a harlot of the city of Gaza. He slept with this prostitute later on after the death of his wife, whom the Philistine had burned (Judges 15:6).

> *One day Samson went to the Philistine city of Gaza and spent the night with a prostitute. Word soon spread that Samson was there, so the men of Gaza gathered together and waited all night at the city gates. They kept quiet during the night, saying to themselves, "When the light of morning comes, we will kill him." But Samson stayed in bed only until midnight. Then he got up, took hold of the city gates with its two posts, and lifted them, bar and all, right out of*

> *the ground. He put them on his shoulders and carried them all the way to the top of the hill across from Hebron.*
> Judges 16:1–3 (NLT)

No offence ya'll, but Samson must have been a brother. He was too cool and too smooth in his mess. You know, I notice that every time Samson fought with the Philistines, the Spirit of the Lord would come upon him mightily. Every time he fought the Philistines, the fury of God would move. But the night he slept with the harlot, the scriptures says nothing about the Spirit of Lord moving. Does this mean God approved of his behavior with the harlot? Absolutely not! I am sure Samson got away with a lot of things in his lifetime. No matter what Samson may have done, the Lord was going to finish what he started. He knew what Samson would do, when he sent him.

Samson got up from sleeping with a prostitute and ripped those bars out of the ground and went about his business. He was always hanging around the Philistines' women, putting himself in harm's way. Like so many of the Lord's Christians do today. Eventually it caught up with Samson, but the Lord was using him as instrument to wipe out the Philistines. Fellas! Gals! Who's using you? The Lord, or Satan?

The third Philistine woman Samson became involved with was Delilah, meaning *"long hair hanging down and weak."* Now if that doesn't sound like she had a part to play in Samson's destiny, I don't know what does. It was her lap that Samson laid his head when his long hair was cut off. I have elaborated on the meaning of names in one of my upcoming books, *Destiny Hidden in a Name*.

Delilah was used by her own people, causing Samson not only to lose his hair but his eyes too. This time his ways had caught up with him. She caused him to fall asleep on her lap.

> *Delilah lulled Samson to sleep with his head in her lap and she called in a man to shave off his hair, making his capture certain. And his strength left him. Then she cried out, "Samson! The Philistines have come to capture you!" When he woke up he thought, "I will do as before and shake myself free." But he didn't realize the Lord had left him. So the Philistines captured him and gouged out his eyes. They then took him to Gaza where he was bound with bronze chains and made to grind in the prison. But before long his hair began to grow back.*
>
> Judges 16:19–22 (NLT)

Samson regained his strength, but he never regained his sight. In the end, he gave up his own life. After Delilah helped the Philistines captured Samson, he prayed that God would give him the strength to judge the Philistines one more time for destroying his eyes and he asked God to let him die with them. Could it be that Samson asked to die with the Philistines, because they had taken his eyes and he didn't want to live that way? I believe it was. Otherwise, when the power of God came upon him to bring down the arena, crushing the Philistines, that same power would have caused him to walk right out of that rubble. God answered Samson's prayer and God's purpose for sending Samson was fulfilled.

> *Then Samson prayed to the Lord, "Sovereign Lord, remember me again. O God, please strengthen me one more time so that I may pay back the Philistines for the loss of my eyes." Then Samson put his hands on the center pillars of the temple and pushed against them with all his might. "Let me die with the Philistines," he prayed. And the temple crashed down on the Philistine leaders and all the people. So he killed more people when he died than he had during his entire lifetime. Later his brothers and other relatives went down to get his body.*

> *They took him back home and buried him between Zorah and Eshtaol where his father Manoah was buried. Samson had been Israel's judge for twenty years.*
>
> Judges 16:28 (NLT)

Though Samson's life seen to have ended tragically; his purpose on earth was fulfilled. We can see that Samson really did fulfill his life's destiny, which was to judge the Philistines for oppressing the children of Israel. God sent him into the world to do just that, and he did. He killed thirty men of Ashkelon, he took three hundred foxes and burned down their fields, he slaughtered many more of them for burning his wife and father-in-law, he killed one thousand Philistines with a donkey's jawbone and he killed thousands more at the end of his life, than he did during his entire lifetime.

The Philistine leaders and all the Philistine people of the land, gathered to celebrate and give offerings to their so-called god, Dagon, for the capture of Samson. So they thought! They said, "Our god Dagon has given us victory over our enemy. Our gods have delivered our enemy to us." And they became drunk and gave praises and sacrifices to their so-called gods.

Now is that any way to honor a god? Well, I guess that would depend on who he or she is, huh? Especially when they are just an idol made with human hands. There is only one God. God means "Supreme Ruler," so how can there be more than one? There is only one Creator. All other so-called gods made by human hands are simply idols, just as the Almighty God says. But the "I AM God" was not made by human hands. He created the heavens and the earth and everything beneath it.

> *The wisest of people who worship idols are stupid and foolish. The things they worship are made of wood! They*

> *bring beaten sheets of silver from Tarshish and gold from Uphaz, and they give these materials to skillful craftsmen who make their idols. Then they dress these gods in royal purple robes made by expert tailors. But the LORD is the only true God, the living God. He is the everlasting King! The whole earth trembles at his anger. The nations hide before his wrath. Say this to those who worship other gods: "Your so-called gods, who did not make the heavens and earth, will vanish from the earth."*
> Jeremiah 10:8–11 (NLT)

Dagon was an idol god of the Philistines, whose name meant "little fish," or "Diar." He was a mythological god, adopted of their belief system. They believed he was a man and half fish. The Babylonians believed a being emerged from the Erythraean Sea and that he was part fish and part man, so their culture adopted this mythical belief. The Philistines ranted and raided about how their god Dagon delivered Samson into their hands. It wasn't their god that delivered Samson. They paid Delilah, a Philistine woman whom Samson loved, to deceive him to get the secret of his strength in order that they themselves could capture him. Their god, which was made of stone, could not move, think, act, or speak.

Delilah received payment for tricking Samson, because she didn't love him, but he certainly loved her. The Scriptures stated that Samson loved Delilah, but never said that she loved him. I believe if she really did, she wouldn't have betrayed him. She may have also feared the Philistines leaders because of what they did to Samson's wife and father-in-law. She forsook Samson like the other Philistine woman whom Samson married. Both women betrayed his love and trust to the Philistines. His wife of Timnah betrayed him because she feared for her life and her father's life. Though his wife gave them the answer to his riddle; consequently, they still lost their lives. Delilah betrayed Samson love for money.

The Holy Spirit also taught me this. Both of these women nagged Samson until he finally gave in to them. When he did this, his enemies were able to defeat him. He showed me that when a wife constantly nags her husband, she can weaken him to the point that his enemies can defeat him. Though it may seem impossible not to nag, it can be overcome. Women hate nagging as much as men, so give it up girls, because it never accomplishes anything good in the end.

> *A nagging wife is as annoying as the constant dripping on a rainy day. Trying to stop her complaints is like trying to stop the wind or hold something with greased hands.*
> Proverbs 27:15–16 (NLT)

Love will always protect you, and it will not betray or deceive you. A woman who loves you will help strengthen you, not zap it from you. A word to the men here! A woman in the hand of God will bring you life and peace. According to King Solomon, she will be good to you, all the days of your life. But a woman in the hand of the Satan will bring death, hell, and destruction. So, be sure the woman whose lap you lay your head upon, loves you or she might cause you to lose something too.

> *The lips of an immoral woman are as sweet as honey, and her mouth is smoother than oil. But the result is as bitter as poison, sharp as a double-edged sword. Her feet go down to death; her steps lead straight to the grave.*
> Proverbs 5:3–5 (NLT)

> *Who can find a virtuous woman? For her price is far above rubies. The heart of her husband doth safely trust in her, so that he shall have no need of spoil. She will do him good and not evil all the days of her life.*
>
> Proverbs 31:10–12 (KJV)

Again, I say, it was not the gods of the Philistines that caused them to capture Samson, but it was their own evil little plot that led to Samson's capture. Moreover, the God of our fathers Abraham, Isaac and Jacob allowed it, so he could accomplish his judgment on them. Samson's strength did not lie within his hair as most people have been taught and believed. His long hair symbolized who he was—a Nazarite unto God, set apart for God's use. It was the power of God upon Samson that made him incredibly strong. The Lord didn't forsake Samson because some woman deceived him. Nor did he ever say to Samson in the Scriptures, *don't ever tell anyone about our little secret.* No! The Lord said before his birth, he had a plan for Samson's life. He said, I will use Samson to judge the nation of the Philistine for oppressing the children of Israel. Remember when Samson first told his parents he wanted to marry the first Philistine woman, before Delilah came on the scene—the one that was burned in her home with her father. The Scriptures said it was of the Lord that Samson wanted her. The Lord was preparing a way to judge the Philistines.

> *His father and mother objected strenuously, "Isn't there one woman in our tribe or among all the Israelites you could marry? Why must you go to the pagan Philistines to find a wife?" But Samson told his father, "Get her for me. She is the one I want." His father and mother didn't realize*

> *the LORD was at work in this, creating an opportunity to disrupt the Philistines, who ruled over Israel at that time.*
>
> Judges 14:3–4 (NLT)

When God was ready to act, his Spirit would come upon Samson, using him to wipe out the Philistines at different times. Delilah was another instrument God used to finish his judgment against the Philistine nation. Please note, too, that God doesn't go around judging a people for nothing. God gives plenty of warnings and time to repent. Like he did for the people of Nineveh, who repented after Jonah warned them of God's judgment, because of their sins (Jonah 3:5–10).

The Philistine lords used Delilah as a weapon to capture Samson, but in all actuality, God used Samson as his weapon in capturing the Philistines and judging them once and for all. It was his final act against the Philistines. God is the one who is in control, not the Philistines, or the false gods they worshipped, or Delilah. Samson's whole purpose for living was because God had sent him into the world at his appointed time and purpose. He was God's instrument to destroy the Philistines for oppressing the lives of God's people. I believed it grieved the Lord to see Samson lose his eyes and later asked to die with the Philistines because of it. Nevertheless, he honored Samson's prayer and somewhere in God's recorded books concerning our lives, near Samson's name it probably says, "Mission accomplished!"

> *Then Samson put his hands on the center pillars of the temple and pushed against them with all his might. "Let me die with the Philistines," he prayed. And the temple crashed down on the Philistine leaders and all the people. So he killed more people when he died than he had during his entire lifetime.*
>
> Judges 16:28–30 (NLT)

My friend Stephen and I were discussing the life of Samson one day, and he asked me, "What do you think was the moral of the story of Samson and Delilah?"

I told him, "If Samson's life was about his affair with women, most people would say, 'Never trust a woman,' but that would not be fair or accurate. It depends on what kind of woman she is." Delilah was ungodly. Nor did she believe in the true and living God, but she believed in false gods and worshipped them. She loved money more than life. That kind you definitely shouldn't trust or choose for a wife. But a virtuous woman will do what is good and right unto her husband, all the days of his life. Would she be flawless? No. But she will strive to do what is right for him as well as for her.

Moreover, Samson's life was not just about his relationship with a woman named Delilah. Delilah was only a fraction of it that eventually led to the end part of his life. Though Samson's life was full of activities with women, the Almighty God still used him. The life of Samson was about a man God sent into the earth to fulfill a mandate—to judge the nation of the Philistines for oppressing the people of God.

Samson's father, named Manoah, was a descendent of the tribe of Dan. Dan was one of the twelve sons of Israel (Jacob). Dan means *"judge."* Samson's life was preplanned by God to represent him as judge over the children of Israel. So to answer the question, the moral of the story is: "It is evidently clear, that God indeed has a pre-planned purpose for sending a life. With sovereignty and justice he delivers and fulfills his plans for us. He judges those who oppress another individual or a people. And he uses whatever and whomever he chooses to do it, in spite of their weaknesses and failures. And for God to get a job done, it only takes ONE!"

Child-Less

> *But Jesus turned and said to them, "Daughters of Jerusalem, don't weep for me, but weep for yourselves and for your children. For the days are coming when they will say, 'Fortunate indeed are the women who are childless, the wombs that have not borne a child and the breasts that have never nursed.'*
>
> Luke 23:28-29 (NLT)

When I was a very young girl, I dreamed of having a family. I have always wanted a good husband, one who would love me and our children. But I never had any children. During junior high school, we had to watch a film on delivering children and it frightened me to see it. I guess I wasn't ready for it. The labor pain, the blood and all that the women had to go through. I thought to myself then, *I'm not having children.*

As time went on, I start saying, *I'm never going to have children. I'll adopt them.* I said this, because I was still afraid. Finally, I got married, but I was still afraid to have children. I told my ex-husband let's wait for about 5 years, giving us time to get some things accomplished. Five years turned into eight, eight into ten, ten into 15 and 15 into a divorce. No, the fact that I didn't want children did not cause the divorce. He was quite content, because he had three from a previous relationship. Nor was it our sex life. It was great! In fact, that was the last thing to die before the divorce. In case my future husband is reading this, I want to make this very clear. I said our sex-life died, not my sex drive. It is alive and well.

Now that I am no longer married, I had to put that drive in park. Hopefully, the Lord will send me the husband of his heart and my dream. I must admit it looks pretty bleak to me, due to the bombardment of sexual immorality and fewer men willing to take on man's greatest challenge—commitment in holy matrimony to one wife for life. I know a lot of women who were faithful to their husband when they were married, but I can't say that about one husband. And they say men like a challenge! Well, I've got a real challenge for all the players. Repent and return home to the one you belong and to the rest of you single players, get right, get a wife and love her for the rest of your life. Now there's a real challenge for you.

Today millions of men and women have made sexual immorality a career. Children are taught to be promiscuous, even in our school systems, rather than remaining pure until marriage. The leaders of our nation no longer band obscene and indecent exposure or behaviors, instead they promote it. Certain educated judges argue back and forth over what is obscene and what is free speech. The dictionary meaning for obscene is, "Offensive to morality or decency." or "To cause uncontrollable sex desires" "Abominable" "disgusting" and "repulsive."

Indecency means, "The state or quality of being unseemly or immodest." Case closed!"

> *And don't forget the cities of Sodom and Gomorrah and their neighboring towns, which were filled with sexual immorality and every kind of sexual perversion. Those cities were destroyed by fire and are a warning of the eternal fire that will punish all who are evil.*
>
> Jude 7:7(NLT)

Our networks and radios are saturated with sexual programs, sexual products for men and all other kinds of sexual material promoting sexual immorality as if they are selling a food product. Nothing is regulated anymore. Studies show that infidelity hit an all time high when products like Viagra were produced. I'm not knocking it if it helps to enhance intimacy between a husband and a wife, but I am when it comes to committing adultery.

God has not changed his mind concerning adultery, fornication, and any other form of sexually immorality. Anything apart from a covenant marriage between a man and a woman, God still judges it. He hates sexual immorality so much that he sent a plague among the children of Israel killing 24,000 people. But when one man took a bold stand against it, the Lord stopped the plague and made a covenant of everlasting peace with him.

> *The LORD issued the following command to Moses: "Seize all the ringleaders and execute them before the LORD in broad daylight, so his fierce anger will turn away from the people of Israel." So Moses ordered Israel's judges to execute everyone who had joined in worshiping Baal of Peor. Just then one of the Israelite men brought a Midianite woman into the camp, right before the eyes of Moses and all the people, as they were weeping at the entrance of the*

> *Tabernacle. When Phinehas son of Eleazar and grandson of Aaron the priest saw this, he jumped up and left the assembly. Then he took a spear and rushed after the man into his tent. Phinehas thrust the spear all the way through the man's body and into the woman's stomach. So the plague against the Israelites was stopped, but not before 24,000 people had died. Then the LORD said to Moses, "Phinehas son of Eleazar and grandson of Aaron the priest has turned my anger away from the Israelites by displaying passionate zeal among them on my behalf. So I have stopped destroying all Israel as I had intended to do in my anger. So tell him that I am making my special covenant of peace with him. In this covenant, he and his descendants will be priests for all time, because he was zealous for his God and made atonement for the people of Israel."*
>
> Numbers 25:4–13(NLT)

Can you imagine what it must have looked like as the people stood by watching them bring their bodies from out of the tent? Doesn't this prove how much God hates sexual immorality?

The children of Israel realized they were under the judgment of God and they knew why. But when our nation is faced with a horrific hurricane like Katrina, or wildfires and plagues, people reject it as being judgment from God and they explain it away.

The Lord was very angry concerning their sin, but he wasn't angry at Phinehas for killing two people indulging in sexual immorality. Instead the Lord rewarded him for the passionate zeal he displayed against it. God made a covenant of peace with Phinehas and his descendants forever. I don't know who they are, but those descendants are walking in that covenant of peace today. Phinehas was a Priest and the man he killed was a leader and the woman was the daughter of a leader.

> *The Israelite man killed with the Midianite woman was named Zimri son of Salu, the leader of a family from the tribe of Simeon. The woman's name was Cozbi; she was the daughter of Zur, the leader of a Midianite clan. Then the LORD said to Moses, "Attack the Midianites and destroy them, because they assaulted you with deceit by tricking you into worshiping Baal of Peor, and because of Cozbi, the daughter of a Midianite leader, who was killed on the day of the plague at Peor."*
> Num 25:14–18(NLT)

Now what if more of our church leaders stood as he did today? I'm not saying that they should go around spearing those who are guilty of this in the back, but rather having the same kind of zeal in their hearts, their messages and their stands against our congressional leaders and corporations concerning these things, and other corruptions that brings the judgment of God on our nation.

I believe if this passage along had been taught down through the years, there would not be such a free range of sexual activity on our networks, in songs, or in our society. There would have been fewer divorces, fewer rapes, fewer young people living promiscuously and child molesters or pedophiles would be almost unheard of. And we wouldn't be arguing with our government that our tax dollars be not use to fund abortions.

Our nation's leaders would set greater examples of faithfulness and adultery would be less likely to happen. And sexual transmitted diseases and all the things mentioned above would hardly be mentioned among the body of Christ. Because our leadership has allowed the freedom of sexual immorality to saturate our networks and Internet, it has aided in the ruins of many marriages and lives. Instead of bombarding congress to clean up the airways, many Christians sit idly by letting it happen and others put a bandage over the problems, rather than taking a strong stand with the few Christian organizations who are fighting to kill the problem at the root.

Infidelity and sexually transmitted diseases are just as rampant among Christians as it is among Non-Christians. As for getting married, sometimes I feel maybe the Lord has not sent some of us a husband, because he wants to prevent us from having our hearts torn apart over and over again.

I was lying back on my bed one evening feeling very lonely and I poured out my heart to the Lord. Very adamantly I asked, *"Lord, do you want me to marry or not?"* Then I heard these words very clearly. *"Jeremiah 16:2."* So I sat up and said, *"ok, let me read and see what it says."* I flipped right to it and it says:

> *"Do not marry or have children in this place. For this is what the* LORD *says about the children born here in this city and about their mothers and fathers: They will die from terrible diseases. No one will mourn for them or bury them, and they will lie scattered on the ground like dung. They will die from war and famine, and their bodies will be food for the vultures and wild animals.*
>
> Jeremiah 16:2–4(NLT)

I was shocked! I couldn't believe my eyes. I said, *"Are you saying this to me or were you just talking to Jeremiah?"* Then I said, *"Ok Lord! You told him not to marry in that city. He must have married some other time."* So then I read through the entire book of Jeremiah, combing through it hoping to see where he later married, but I never found it. Talk about a broken heart! I still find myself thinking today, maybe he married later in life and the word of God just didn't record it. I also find myself reasoning with the Lord over whether he means for me to not marry in this city, in this country, or in the world. I definitely want God's best for me. Nevertheless, if it is not his will for me to marry, I will remain hopeful for you. I still believe it is possible for God to send a husband to the women who still desire to be married.

> *"May the LORD bless you with the security of another marriage."*
> Ruth 1:9a (NLT)

There were other things that played into the equation of not wanting to have children. Being self employed and no help, there were many nights when I worked without having any sleep. So I didn't see how I could possibly raise children well. I admire the many single mothers working and raising their kids alone, because I know it's hard. I see and talk with them all the time. In fact, it's a miracle, considering the cost of living today. It also grieves me to see so many men letting them go through the struggle of raising their own children. Some of these women work 2 to 3 jobs to provide the expenses needed to put a decent roof over their heads and everything else these dads, won't do, for their own flesh and blood.

Although my ex-husband would have played well with our children, after a few years of marriage, I knew, the financial responsibility would have been greatly upon me. Had I had them, I would not want our children to see or believe that is the way it is suppose to be. I wanted my children to have a father who would help me teach them how to live according to the word of God and bring the blessings of God upon their lives. I wasn't looking for a perfect husband or a perfect home, but a husband who loves the Lord, who would love me and our children. I wanted someone to help provide a home of safety, godliness, unity, peace and happiness.

> *Live happily with the woman you love through all the meaningless days of life that God has given you in this world. The wife God gives you is your reward for all your earthly toil.*
> Ecclesiastes 9:9–10 (NLT)

> *So again I say, each man must love his wife as he loves himself, and the wife must respect her husband.*
> Ephesians 5:33 (NLT)

As I continue to see all the troubles, the sorrows, the struggles, the dangers, and the evils in our world, the less I wanted children. I didn't want them raised in a home where they would be exposed to a lifestyle of alcohol, cigarettes or other substance abuse. I didn't want them hearing us fusing over entertainment that wasn't appropriate for Christians. Nor the constant promotion of promiscuous living, obscene and indecent exposure and all other forms of sexual immorality, seen from the U.S. White House, to the Lord's house, to the school house. All these things wreck lives.

> *Again I observed all the oppression that takes place in our world. I saw the tears of the oppressed, with no one to comfort them. The oppressors have great power, and the victims are helpless. So I concluded that the dead are better off than the living. And most fortunate of all are those who were never born. For they have never seen all the evil that is done in our world.*
> Ecclesiastes 4:1–3 (NLT)

Am I saying I never used or did such things? Certainly not! I was once guilty too. But I learned better and wanted better. When I renewed my relationship with the Lord on January 8th 1984, an amazing thing took place in me that day. But just a week before I renewed my relationship, I was standing on the sidewalk of downtown Beale St. here in Memphis, Tn. At this time I was 23 years of age. It was December 31, 1983 just hours from New Year's Day and I was partying with a few friends. I had been smoking and drinking alcohol when all of a sudden, I looked all around me and everything looked so strange, like I was watching a film. People were walking and partying and I just stood there looking. I sensed in me at that very moment, this was not the life I wanted to live, nor was I raised to live. It appeared I was having fun, but inside of me I felt empty, lonely and unfulfilled. I didn't mention what I was feeling or thinking to anyone. Nor did I go home right away, but I stood there and I spoke to the Lord. I can't remember if I spoke aloud or in my mind, but I said, *"Lord I'm going to party this one last time and then I am going to give my life to you."* In my heart I really meant that. Thank God, his grace kept me, and he helped me to keep my promise a week later.

When my girl friend called the next weekend to go out, I told her no, I am not going, because if I do I won't get up and go to church. I told her I had been telling my brother Rickey for weeks that I would go with him to church, but every time he woke me, I said I was too tired and that Sunday was the only morning I could get extra sleep. So that weekend I stayed home and when Rickey woke me up, I went to church with him and gave my life back to the Lord and he filled my heart with so much love, joy and peace. I was so happy, as soon as I saw my mother, I said "Momma, guess what happened to me today? I got saved!"

> *For if you confess with your mouth that Jesus is Lord and believe in your heart that God raised him from the dead, you will be saved. For it is by believing in your heart that you are made right with God, and it is by confessing with your mouth that you are saved. As the Scriptures tell us, "Anyone who believes in him will not be disappointed." Jew and Gentile*

> are the same in this respect. They all have the same Lord, who generously gives his riches to all who ask for them. For "Anyone who calls on the name of the Lord will be saved."
> Roman 10:9–13 (NLT)

From that Sunday, January 8th 1984, I had no desire for drinking and partying anymore. I left services that afternoon with a great hunger for God and all I wanted was to learn more about the Lord and his word. When Sunday service was over, I couldn't wait for Wednesday night Bible study. When that was over, I couldn't wait for Friday night Bible study. When that was over, I couldn't wait for Sunday again. I would lie on the floor of my living-room and read the Bible for hours. Three years later after I got married, my husband, who I am no longer married to, we had to share a car. Whenever he wanted to keep the car, he would drop me off 4 hours early, because he had to be at work at 6:00 am. Many of those mornings I would lay in the floor at work and read my Bible until around 9:00 a.m. Then I would get up and open the doors for business. When I kept the car, rather than go all the way back home, I sat and ate breakfast across from the shop and read my Bible until it was time to open the shop.

> *I will give you a new heart and put a new spirit within you; I will take the heart of stone out of your flesh and give you a heart of flesh. I will put My Spirit within you and cause you to walk in My statutes, and you will keep My judgments and do them.*
> Ezekiel 36:26–28 (NKJV)

Although I was hungry for the Lord, there was one thing still clinging to me. Cigarettes! Virginia Slim/Menthol 100s! And though in my heart I didn't want to smoke anymore, I continued to do so. I prayed several times asking the Lord to help me to quit. By this time a year had passed and I was attending Morning Star Holiness Church. It bothered me so much to know smoking was hurting my testimony as a Christian, till one day, I went on a 2 week fast with my church. The fast started at 12 midnight until 3:00 p.m. each day, for 2 weeks. I prayed earnestly that the Lord would help me to quit, because it was hurting my testimony for Christ.

Before the 2nd week was up, the desire was completely gone. I didn't even realize it, until I smelt the smoke of a cigarette a customer lit, just before he walked out the door. I didn't see him light it because I was busy putting away his order. Then I thought to myself, *what is that smell?* When I lifted my head I saw the smoke lingering in the air as he walked out the door. Oh Boy, did I rejoice! It was then that I realized, I hadn't thought, nor wanted a cigarette in 3 days. That was over 22 years ago and I have not wanted or touched a cigarette since. Halleluiah! Praise God and his son Jesus.

So no, I was not innocent, of these things. But when the Lord forgave me, I wanted to live better and have better. Concerning having children. Maybe it was selfishness that prevented me too from having children. Maybe it was my deep down fear and my confession not to have them. Maybe it was medical, because after 15 years of marriage and having never used birth control, I never conceived. Being content, I never tried to see if it was medical or not. All I know is I never became pregnant.

Children are a blessing from the Lord and they give you another reason to love and live for someone else, other than for self. After many years have passed and not having to raise one child, I've fallen short of the patience needed to raise them now. Several years ago, as I dwell on all this, and my desire for a Godly husband and the little girl I always wanted, but never had, I wrote this poem.

CHILD-LESS

If you were my child, what would I do?
I would praise and thank God for giving me you.
I'd love you so much, hold you gently tight,
Listening for your voice, throughout the day and night;
Nurture you, protect you, and chase away your fears,
Letting you know, mother's love is always here.
I'll not scream in your face, nor shout in your ears,
But touch and embrace you, and wipe away your tears.
What a small miracle, to hold you in my arms,
Loving and embracing you, while keeping you warm.
Gazing into your eyes, kissing your little face;
Whispering in your ears sweet melodies of grace.
O' there will be time for discipline too,
But with loving-kindness I'll do this, because I love you.
If your wounds are physical, I will bandage them up,
If they are spiritual, I will speak words of grace, not corrupt.
I'll teach and show you some of the finer things in life,
Through believing and doing what God says is right.
You'll see things that are not so good and fair,
So you will appreciate what you have, learning to give and to share.
You'll learn God's way versus life's follies and games,
So you'll know how to recognize the real and true things.
You'll know and enjoy the highest form of life,
That can only be obtained through the Lord Jesus Christ.
I'll teach you to know and to understand,
You were created for God's holy plan.
Oh how blessed your life would be,
As you live to please God, not man and not me;
Your life would be filled with pleasant sweet rain,
Not hell on earth that bring such pain.
Of course, there will be tests and trials too,
But God gives comfort and wisdom in what to do.
To teach you to give and receive love; Oh! The joy that will bring;
And I will help you to understand when life seems so mean.
You'll learn to be patient and let love find you;
This will prevent heartaches and days of blue.

God's Appointed Destiny

I'll encourage you to wait on God's appointed mate for you to marry,
And take on no burden, not meant for you to carry.
I'll teach you to give and bring healing to a hurting heart,
These are eternal things that greatly please God.
O' I heard 'em say, "she doesn't have a child,
how'd she know what to do or to say?"
Well, I tell you this, I've learned how to love, and I know how to pray.
And I've seen and heard the grieves and pains of my sisters and brothers;
And some of life's greatest experiences, are what we learn from others.
Not only that, I too have seen the world from the eyes of a child;
How they act, how they think, how they hurt and how they smile.
I've shed a child's diamond size tears,
Seen bones broken and I've had scars healed.
When people looked big, accept my little peers,
And when things seemed far, time seemed forever and weeks like years.
Most of all I have eyes, ears, hands and a heart;
The Spirit of wisdom and the love of God;
Yes............I know what to say and do;
And what I don't know, I will learn that too.
If you were my child, I would lavish all these gifts on you,
And not just on my child, but the child of others, too.
Moreover, concerning you, one of my greatest prayers would be,
That you live a long and fulfilling life and more abundantly;
Because of God's grace, my days are not blue,
I've accepted the fact that I never bore you.
But in God's time should you arrive,
There's one thing above all, I'll greatly ask you to try;
The love of the True and Living God and to love yourself,
By this, you will learn to love life and everyone else.

—Be'Trice Ronique Jenkins Donald

A Reason and A Season

To everything there is a season, a time for every purpose under heaven: a time to be born, and a time to die.
Ecclesiastes 3:1–2 (NKJV)

To every life on earth, God indeed has appointed a special purpose. Parents or guardians can and should know their purpose and their children's purpose. The Lord is going to hold each parent accountable for the children he has given them. If Mr. Williams, the father of Serena and Venus, whom we addressed in chapter two, can say what he and his wife were going to have; and what they are going to be; and see it come to pass. Why not us, who are called by the name of the Almighty God and filled with his Spirit?

The Lord has no respect of persons. God will show you the purpose of your life and that of your child or children if you only ask and believe him. Before they are born you can know. God wants you to know who they are to be, what they are to do, even what to name them. How else are you able to instruct them in the way they are to go as God has commanded if you don't know the call? God doesn't want anyone to live his or her life in vain. Yet there are people who do because they do not know God or his plan concerning their own lives. There are some people who know of him but are not intimate enough with him to know his will for them. Then there are others who know their life's destiny and fulfills it.

In case some of you are thinking this (and I know you are), how about miscarriages or still-born babies? I don't have all the answers, but we do know everything happens for a reason. And as tragic as that is, even this has a reason. Any of you reading this and has experienced this kind of lost, I hope the Lord comforts you and give you peace and assurance that your child is with him. I pray you have taken comfort in knowing you will see him or her and understand all things in time.

One of the main causes of death is sin. Not that the baby sinned, but sometimes it could be because someone else did. God warns us that sin brings death. For example, a pregnant woman may lose a child in a car accident because of a drunk driver, a shooting by an angry person or an abusive husband or boyfriend. It was the sin of those individuals that took the child's life. Sometimes it happens due to the mother's health condition. Today the greatest cause for a child losing their life is due to an abortion. If you have aborted your child, the Lord will forgive you and heal you of the physical and emotional damage it causes.

When these things happen, the powers of darkness, is in play. The word of God says, Satan is the prince of darkness and of this evil world's system and that he works in people who consistently rebel against the will of God. They are also at work trying to tempt the people of God to disobey him, and hinder them from receiving the blessings of God. Millions are influenced by Satan's evil tactics, causing them not to receive the truth of God's word; But God is sovereign, and he knows just when and how to turn people around.

> *For we do not wrestle against flesh and blood, but against principalities, against powers, against the rulers of the darkness of this age, against spiritual hosts of wickedness in the heavenly places.*
> Ephesians 6:12 (NKJV)

We are able to understand these things when we come to the Lord. Some people come to the Lord when they realize just how much he loves them and some come when something drastic happens in their life. Nevertheless, the Lord loves all of us and when we repent, he forgives us no matter how great or small the sin. And he heals and restores us.

Whenever a person sins, it doesn't just affect him, it affects others as well, whether directly or indirectly. Let's say a mother chooses to abort her baby. It was her sin that took the child's life. God had nothing to do with it. He sends the life here with a purpose, but because of mankind's selfishness and sinful heart, a life is taken away.

When people are mislead or have little or no fear of God and little or no regard for human life, they will snuff out a life and think nothing of it. I know there are pro-choice people out there who feel it's your body and you should have the right to do with it whatever you want. Well, I agree! In fact, God has given all of us the freedom to choose what we want to do with our lives and our bodies here in the present and in the future. But the body inside the mother is not her body. That is another body. It is the baby's body. Before a child is conceived in the womb, the Lord God knows them and he has given them life.

> *The LORD gave me a message. He said, "I knew you before I formed you in your mother's womb. Before you were born I set you apart and appointed you as my spokesman to the world."*
> *Jeremiah 1:4–5 (NLT)*

> *You made all the delicate, inner parts of my body and knit me together in my mother's womb. Thank you for making me so wonderfully complex! Your workmanship is marvelous—and how well I know it. You watched me as I was being formed in utter seclusion, as I was woven together in the dark of the womb. You saw me before I was born. Every day of my life was recorded in your book. Every moment was laid out before a single day had passed. How precious are your thoughts about me, O God! They are innumerable!*
> *Psalm 139:13–17 (NLT)*

A man and a woman perform the act that leads to conception, but the Lord is the one who gives life to that act in the womb. That life in the womb of its mother has a choice too. And I'm sure if the baby could speak for him or herself at that time, they would say, "I want to live!"

"I want to fulfill my creative purpose!"

"Please allow me to fulfill my appointed destiny!"

"This world needs me."

"You need me!"

"God has given me a right to live, just like he gave to you!"

"Please don't cut me off!"

As a woman and a man, you do indeed have the right to choose what you do with your body. People do it every day. And should you conceive, you have a choice concerning the life of each child God places in your womb, and the Lord says, "Choose life that you and your children may live." Yes, the choice is yours, and so are the consequences.

I call heaven and earth as witnesses today against you, that I have set before you life and death, blessing and cursing; therefore choose life, that both you and your descendants may live.
Deuteronomy 30:19 (NKJV)

Often the reasons for the lost of a baby before birth or at birth, goes hidden, unless the Lord reveals why. Back up the road someone could have committed a sin, somewhere and somehow that lead to the death of a child. Sometimes, things come back to haunt us because of a sin committed. For example, King David's first baby, born of Bathsheba, lived only 7 days, because he committed adultery with her. David later tried to set up her husband Uriah, to sleep with her so he could pin it on him. When it didn't work, he had him killed on the battlefront. As a result of King David's actions, the baby died. Bathsheba was not at fault, nor the baby, nor the Lord. It was because of David's sinful actions that the baby died.

Then it happened one evening that David arose from his bed and walked on the roof of the king's house. And from the roof he saw a woman bathing, and the woman was very beautiful to behold. So David sent and inquired about the woman. And someone said, "Is this not Bathsheba, the daughter of Eliam, the wife of Uriah the Hittite?" Then David sent messengers, and took her; and she came to him, and he lay with her, for she was cleansed from her impurity; and she returned to her house.
2 Samuel 11:2–4 (NLT)

So David sent word to Joab: "Send me Uriah the Hittite." When Uriah arrived, David asked him how Joab and the army were getting along and how the war was progressing. Then he told Uriah, "Go on home and relax." David even sent a gift to Uriah after he had left the palace. But Uriah

wouldn't go home. He stayed that night at the palace entrance with some of the king's other servants. When David heard what Uriah had done, he summoned him and asked, "What's the matter with you? Why didn't you go home last night after being away for so long?"
2 Samuel 11:6–10 (NLT)

So the next morning David wrote a letter to Joab and gave it to Uriah to deliver. The letter instructed Joab, Station Uriah on the front lines where the battle is fiercest. Then pull back so that he will be killed. So Joab assigned Uriah to a spot close to the city wall where he knew the enemy's strongest men were fighting. And Uriah was killed along with several other Israelite soldiers.
2 Samuel 11:14–17 (NLT)

David begged God to spare the child. He went without food and lay all night on the bare ground. The leaders of the nations pleaded with him to get up and eat with them, but he refused. Then on the seventh day the baby died.
2 Samuel 12:16–18b (NLT)

God is not the one to take life. He gives life. People who sin and rebel against the laws of God take life. Sometimes it's through the physical action of another human being, and sometimes it's through the physical reaction in your own body. Whenever you see the judgment of God that results in taking of life, it has always been because of sin—the sins of an individual, a group, a city, even a whole nation. The Word of God makes it clear that that the wages of sin is death.

For the wages of sin is death; but the gift of God is eternal life through Jesus Christ our Lord.
Romans 6:23 (KJV)

God is good, and he will forgive us if we ask him with repentant hearts. He warns us about the things that can bring death on us, our loved ones, or other innocent victims. God would never punish a child because of the parents' sin. However, the parents' sins can cut off the life of a child or the blessings of children because of the way they lived before them. Not only that, their lifestyles greatly influence their children, just as well as godly parents who live lives of integrity influence their children and set them up to be blessed in life.

> *What? you ask. Doesn't the child pay for the parent's sins? No! For if the child does what is right and keeps my laws, that child will surely live. The one who sins is the one who dies. The child will not be punished for the parent's sins, and the parent will not be punished for the child's sins. Righteous people will be rewarded for their own goodness, and wicked people will be punished for their own wickedness.*
> Ezekiel 18:19–20 (NLT)

> *The godly walk with integrity; blessed are their children after them.*
> Proverbs 20:7 (NLT)

The Lord judged David because his action misrepresented the God of Israel and the God of Righteousness. David acted as if he had done nothing wrong, but God called him to account. He sent the prophet Nathan to David concerning his sin, telling him that he had done a terrible thing and that the result of his sin would never leave his house. David had to deal with the consequences of his sins against God, Urriah and Bathesheba for years, even losing another son Absalom, because he tried to over throw his father's kingship.

Because David quickly repented, the Lord forgave him and blessed David and Bathsheba's next child, named Solomon. In fact, the Word of God says, the Lord loved this child very much. The Lord is not like people who get mad at the parent and hold a grudge against them and the children too. No! He loves us individually. He doesn't love or judge us based on what our parents do but on what we individually do.

The Lord sent the prophet Nathan to them and said name the new baby Jedidiah, meaning *the beloved of the Lord*. It was this son that God made the next king of Israel after the death of his father, even though David had other sons. I believe this particular son of Bathsheba, called Jedidiah (Solomon), was Israel's next king because of God's goodness, mercy, and wisdom. I also believe it was his way of rewarding Bathsheba for the loss of her husband and honoring Uriah's loyalty and his unjust death by letting the son of his wife, whom King David married, become the next king. The results of King David's sin still had to run their course, which ended up affecting his sons, daughters, his wives, and his kingdom.

> *Then David comforted Bath-Sheba, his wife, and slept with her. She became pregnant and gave birth to a son, and they named him Solomon; The Lord loved the child and sent word through Nathan the prophet that his name should be Jedidiah, "beloved of the Lord" because the Lord loved him.*
> 2 Samuel 12:24–25 (NLT)

God loves us, and he loves our children. If there is a problem with carrying a child or children in the womb, God will show us what's going on if we would only ask him. The problem is many times we fail to ask.

Many times, we blame God for the bad things that happen,

but God is good. He's long-suffering, and a loving God of all life. No matter what bad or tragic things may come our way, he will work it out for our good and for his glory.

> *Isaac pleaded with the Lord to give Rebekah a child because she was childless, so the Lord answered Isaac's prayer, and his wife became pregnant with twins. But the two children struggled with each other in her womb. So she asked the Lord about it. Why is this happening to me? she asked. And the Lord told her, The sons in your womb will become two rival nations. One nation will be stronger than the other; the descendants of the older son will serve the descendants of the younger son.*
> Genesis 25:21–23 (NLT)

What may be a secret to one is never a secret to God. This is not to condemn or bring up any past memories of a loss loved one, but to show that there is a purpose in everything and every life, whether good or bad. Even though many times we don't understand why certain things happen, in due time we will. All knowledge and truth, whether good or bad, will be revealed. Thank God, he forgives us whenever we ask him. Remember, God is the author of life, and sin is the author of death.

There was another incident where King Abimelech of the land Gerar took Sarah, the wife of Abraham, into his palace. Even though Abraham led him to believe that she was Abraham's sister, he was about to die.

One night in a dream God appeared to King Abimelech and told him he was a dead man, because he had taken another man's wife. Due to his actions all the women in his palace could not have children. This resulted, even though he didn't know Sarah was married. But God was merciful and showed him what he had done to bring the curse upon his wife and the other women.

> *But God came to Abimelech in a dream by night, and said to him, Indeed you are a dead man because of the woman whom you have taken, for she is a man's wife. But Abimelech had not come near her; and he said, Lord, will You slay a righteous nation also? Did he not say to me, She is my sister? And she, even she herself said, He is my brother. In the integrity of my heart and innocence of my hands I have done this. And God said to him in a dream, Yes, I know that you did this in the integrity of your heart. For I also withheld you from sinning against Me; therefore I did not let you touch her. Now therefore, restore the man's wife; for he is a prophet, and he will pray for you and you shall live. But if you do not restore her, know that you shall surely die, you and all who are yours.*
>
> Genesis 20:3–11 (NKJV)

Do you remember, back in the beginning, when the serpent, called the devil, deceived Eve, and Adam disobeyed God when they ate from the tree of knowledge of good and evil? They opened the door for the curse of sin upon the entire human race. And whose body did the curse come upon? That's right, Eve. God said because of what she did, she would bear children in pain and her husband would rule over her. Adam's punishment was that he would have to toil the land in order that it produce for him.

> *Then he said to the woman, You will bear children with intense pain and suffering. And though your desire will be for your husband, he will be your master. And to Adam he said, Because you listened to your wife and ate the fruit I told you not to eat, I have placed a curse on the ground. All your life you will struggle to scratch a living from it.*
>
> *It will grow thorns and thistles for you, though you will eat of its grains. All your life you will sweat to produce food, until your dying day. Then you will return to the ground*

from which you came. For you were made from dust, and to the dust you will return.
Genesis 3:16–19 (NLT)

Now answer this question. When Aaron and Miriam spoke against Moses, whose body received the punishment, Aaron or Miriam? If you said Miriam, you are right! Miriam was struck with leprosy. Why wasn't Aaron's body affected? "Selah." You think on that!

Now let me tell you what I believe. I believe the Lord wants the man to remain strong because he is the one who has the authority over the women and children; therefore, he has the power to bring them deliverance. Aaron's words along with Miriam got her sick, but Moses' word brought her deliverance. When a man sins against God, his sins affect the wife and children more than anyone else.

This may be even harder to swallow, but most sexually transmitted diseases a woman or young girl contracts are contracted from a man. There is no way it can make its way into her vagina unless some man put it there. I am not talking about a blood transfusion—that is the fault of medical science. I'm talking about when a wife, a woman, or a young girl finds out she contracted a sexually transmitted disease. A man transmitted it there. Even before she could pass it on, it was transferred to her first. That's how much damage a man can do when he is out of order and unfaithful. It also shows the power man has to make and keep things right if he will consistently walk in his God-ordained position.

> *The people of the land have used oppressions, committed robbery, and mistreated the poor and needy; and they wrongfully oppress the stranger. So I sought for a man among them who would make a wall, and stand in the gap*

> *before Me on behalf of the land, that I should not destroy it; but I found no one. Therefore I have poured out My indignation on them; I have consumed them with the fire of My wrath; and I have recompensed their deeds on their own heads," says the Lord God.*
> Ezekiel 22:29–31 (NKJV)

When men disobey God, it indeed affects their women and children too. When a king sins, his wife is affected, even his entire kingdom. When a president sins, it affects his country; when a member of the house of Congress sins, it affects his role in government and his family; when a governor sins, it affects his state; when a mayor sins, it affects his city; when a CEO sins, it affect his company and its customers; when a husband sins, it affects his family; when a pastor sins, it affects his ministry, the body of Christ, and the name of our God, and so forth. That goes for women leaders too. So no more saying, *What I do only affects me.* That is not true!

Now, for all you folks who said you didn't know he or she was married. Remember, God knows. If you don't know, he will cause you to find out. Once you know, it's up to you to do the right thing. Thank God, he will forgive us when we repent with a sincere heart. And remember, we can't hide from God.

> *Don't try to avoid responsibility by saying you didn't know about it. For God knows all hearts, and he sees you. He keeps watch over your soul, and he knows you knew! And he will judge all people according to what they have done.*
> Proverbs 24:12 (NLT)

Wow! All that's said in one verse! And you can't get any clearer than that. So, just repent. He knows you knew.

Then there was Michal, the wife of King David, who rebuked him for dancing and praising God before all the people, especially the women. Because of her attitude toward her husband, the Lord shut her womb, and she later lost her position as David's wife and was given to another man to marry. Even after that, she was still never able to have children. I believe if she had repented, God would have opened her womb again just as he did for all the women in the house of Abimelech, but there is no record of her asking God to forgive her. And we all know that God would have because he is a forgiving God and he has no respect of persons.

> *Now as the ark of the Lord came into the City of David, Michal, Saul's daughter, looked through a window and saw King David leaping and whirling before the Lord; and she despised him in her heart. So they brought the ark of the Lord, and set it in its place in the midst of the tabernacle that David had erected for it. Then David offered burnt offerings and peace offerings before the Lord. And when David had finished offering burnt offerings and peace offerings, he blessed the people in the name of the Lord of hosts.*
>
> 2 Samuel 6:16–18 (NKJV)

> *Then David returned to bless his household. And Michal the daughter of Saul came out to meet David, and said, How glorious was the king of Israel today, uncovering himself today in the eyes of the maids of his servants, as one of the base fellows shamelessly uncovers himself! So David said to Michal, It was before the Lord, who chose me instead of your father and all his house, to appoint me ruler over the people of the Lord, over Israel. Therefore I will play music before the Lord. And I will be even more undignified than this, and will be humble in my own sight. But as for the maidservants of whom you have spoken, by them I will be*

held in honor. Therefore Michal the daughter of Saul had no children to the day of her death.
2 Samuel 6:20–23 (NKJV)

Some of you may even be wondering about women who never had children yet wanted them. God is sovereign, and he may not give them at the time asked. But he will give them at the appointed time, if we don't give up. He did it for Rebekkah, Hannah, Rachel, Monnaoh's wife, Sarah, the wife of Abraham, and for Elizabeth, the wife of Zechariah. Some of you reading this book right now know couples who struggled and anguished for a child, but in time God will answer. For these couples it looked hopeless, but the child arrived at God's appointed time.

Two of these couples, Abraham and Sarah, also Zechariah and Elizabeth, were very old when they had children. You see, it's not that God doesn't want you to have children. It very well could be for an appointed time. He sends children in the earth to fulfill a purpose that will need filling in their lifetime and for generations to come. Then there are others the Lord gives children to through adoption because he knows those parents will help him raise those children to fulfill what he wants them to do. Just because a mother gives her child up for adoption, it does not abort the plan of God on that child's life.

Life does indeed bring with it much trouble, pain, and sorrow, often caused by our sins and the sins of others, and children are the ones who suffer the most. Children are innocent, and they all need guidance. They need guidance that leads to life, not death. But due to selfishness, greed, laziness, hatred etc., many of them are broken and abused, and millions of others, murdered. But there is coming a day appointed to those who have done such things and never repented. And there is a day appointed to all those who know and love the Lord, when he will wipe away all tears, pain, and sorrows forever, and there will be joy and peace forevermore. However, until then, please remember, the Lord our God is with us, and he keeps records.

The Lord doesn't haphazardly do things. God is the all-wise God, and he is sovereign. He is in control of all things. He does everything for and with a purpose, at the appointed time.

So he will do for me all he has planned. He controls my destiny.

Job 23:14 (NLT)

Purposely Designed after Its Own Kind

And God made the beast of the earth according to its kind, cattle according to its kind, and everything that creeps on the earth according to its kind. And God saw that it was good. Then God said, "Let Us make man in Our image, according to Our likeness; let them have dominion over the fish of the sea, over the birds of the air, and over the cattle, over all the earth and over every creeping thing that creeps on the earth." So God created man in His own image; in the image of God He created him; male and female He created them. Then God blessed them, and God said to them, "Be fruitful and multiply; fill the earth and subdue it; have dominion over the fish of the sea, over the birds of the air, and over every living thing that moves on the earth."

Genesis 1:25–28 (NKJV)

The Creator of life is not unknown or confusing. God has put it in man to know that he exist. The knowledge of God is only rejected by those who choose to rebel against what God has already revealed in their hearts. God Most High himself created man with an awareness that he is, and he has even placed a knowing of eternity in every human heart. That's why industries are always looking for ways to help people live longer and be more youthful. It's our longing for eternity that makes us want to live long, healthy lives, full of vitality.

> *He has made everything beautiful in its time. Also He has put eternity in their hearts, except that no one can find out the work that God does from beginning to end.*
> Ecclesiastes 3:11 (NKJV)

The soul of man will live on forever. The more important matter concerning his eternal existence is not how, but where, he will spend it. Will it be in eternal death or in eternal life? God the Father owns eternity, and Jesus, the Son of God, is the entrance to it.

> *And this is what God has testified: He has given us eternal life, and this life is in his Son. So whoever has God's Son has life; whoever does not have his Son does not have life.*
> 1 John 5:11–12 (NLT)

> *Jesus said to him, "I am the way, the truth, and the life. No one comes to the Father except through Me."*
> John 14:6 (NKJV)

> *We know that we are the children of God and that the world around us is under the power and control of the evil one. And we know that the Son of God has come, and he has given us understanding so that we can know the true God. And now we are in God because we are in his Son, Jesus Christ. He is the only true God, and he is eternal life.*
> 1 John 5:19–20 (NLT)

If you want to accept the gift of eternal life the heavenly Father wants for you, then just pray this prayer:

> God of all creation;
> Of the heavens, the earth and everything
> that dwells in it and beneath it.
> I want to be born again.
> You said If I call upon the name of
> the Lord, I shall be saved
> Forgive me of my sins and save me.
> I believe you sent Jesus, your Beloved
> Son, to die for my sins.
> I believe that you raised Jesus from the dead.
> Jesus, I want you to be my Lord and Savior
> and grant me the Gift of Eternal Life.
> Heavenly Father, I ask this in the name
> of Jesus, your only begotten Son;
> Who at this moment is now become
> my Savior, Lord and King;
> And has now given me the Gift of Eternal Life,
> according to Roman 10:9–13:
> Sanctify me in your word and teach
> me your truth by the Holy Spirit
> according to your word in John
> 16:13–14 and John 17:17.
> Teach me to know your ways and
> fulfill your plan for my life.
> Thank you Heavenly Father, In Jesus name, Amen.

For if you confess with your mouth that Jesus is Lord and believe in your heart that God raised him from the dead, you will be saved. For it is by believing in your heart that you are made right with God, and it is by confessing with your mouth that you are saved. As the Scriptures tell us, "Anyone who believes in him will not be disappointed." Jew and Gentile are the same in this respect. They all have the same Lord,

> *who generously gives his riches to all who ask for them. For, "Anyone who calls on the name of the Lord will be saved."*
>
> Romans 10:9–13 (NLT)

I hope you have prayed for forgiveness of your sins through Jesus, the Son of God. If you have, you now have eternal life and your name has been written in the Book of Life. And now that the Spirit of God lives in your heart, you will have a hunger for him. You must begin right away feeding that hunger with the Word of God. And you will experience the sweetest peace and see things through the eyes of the Lord. But you must stay with the Word and it is going to transform your thinking and your life. You will find yourself saying over and over as you began to learn the Word of God, "I wish I had done this long ago!"

The Lord God Almighty has created everything purposefully designed to produce after its kind, after its own likeness and according to its purpose. Whatever the seed is, that is what it will produce. You cannot plant an apple seed and get oranges. That's not the purpose of that seed. The purpose of the apple seed is to produce more apples. If you want oranges, then you have to plant the seed that has that purpose, oranges. Apples beget apples; oranges beget oranges. Oak trees beget oak trees, animals beget animals, people beget people, talents beget talents, and callings beget callings, and so on. The Lord God created everything to reproduce after its own kind.

> *And God said, "Let the earth bring forth every kind of animal—livestock, small animals, and wildlife." And so it was. God made all sorts of wild animals, livestock, and small animals, each able to reproduce more of its own kind. And God saw that it was good.*
>
> Genesis 1:24–25 (NLT)

Now let's take this to the next level—mankind! Mankind was created by God and for his pleasure. Yes, we can give God pleasure instead of pain and disappointment when we live right. The Lord God is a father to those of us who have accepted the death, burial, and resurrection of his son, Jesus. And he wants to be a father to everyone who would believe. Through Jesus he has proven his love for us and his mind is just full of us, he created everything for us to enjoy too. Every good thing, that is! He even assigned his mighty angels to watch over his worldwide creation, just like a city assigns policemen to guard, protect, and keep order.

For He shall give His angels charge over you, To keep you in all your ways.

Psalms 91:11 (NKJV)

God commanded mankind to reproduce and multiply and gave us dominion over all the earth, and everything he created accepted each other.

God never told man to dominate another man. That's oppression, and the Lord doesn't like that. Though many of the men and women of God had servants they were warned of the Lord how to treat them. Some were treated like a member of the family. Sometimes they would inherit their master's possession. Abraham spoke of this when the Lord told him he would have a son. He asked what good was all these blessings if he didn't have a son to inherit it. And that his servant Eliezer would be his heir (Genesis 15:2). Abraham was good to his servants and they were good to him. But those who are cruel and oppress their servant or employees, woe be unto to them.

> *Therefore you shall not oppress one another, but you shall fear your God; for I am the Lord your God.*
>
> Leviticus 25:17 (NKJV)

Mankind was created to dominate the things in the earth, not other mankind. If that scripture isn't enough to put and keep a healthy fear of God in the heart, I don't know what will! God is the Creator, he loves his creation, and he cares for everyone and everything in it. That includes you and me and the birds and the bees, etc. God is a good God. He is loving and faithful and is a defender against those who would do us harm. Now, how could anyone not love a God like this? God loves us so much that he says we are the apple of his eye. Not only that, all of his creation declares his majesty. Time and time again, he has proven himself in his creation and the Lord God loves us very much. He protects and keeps us when we can't even keep ourselves.

Have you ever watched the Discovery Channel showing different kinds of species and how they produce life, how they behave, provide, and protect their own and their environment? It's amazing how the smallest insect thinks and works to survive and give life. They are not confused about what they are so why are we?

I remember during junior high school, there was a picture on the wall showing the stage of man. It was a picture used to teach students the "Evolution Theory" and how man was supposed to have evolved from an ape. It started with an ape and as the figures evolved, it evolved into a tall man. It continued to evolve, until the man was old and bowed over. At this point he had lost about 2 to 3 inches in height, paralleling his height to that of the ape.

As a young teenager I was rather offended at the picture. In fact, I was very hurt about it. I stared at it several times while attending that class. Of course we were taught that was our origin, but it never set well with me. Although those images have become a part of my memory, I thank the Lord he would not allow that theory to become a part of my belief system. I don't remember everything that was taught about this theory, but I do remember thinking, how it never made sense. Even then as a teenager, not understanding a lot about life, the word of God was keeping me.

It's strange that all other species have a reverential sense of their Creator, what they are, and even the common sense to produce from among their own kind, but when it comes to the human species, there is doubt and confusion? Why is it that some human beings, made in the image of God, with the capacity to learn and do far greater than animals, yet they are confused and act as though they have less reverence and knowledge of God? We have the ability to speak and communicate with all nationalities, even animals. And we can reason within the soul and communicate with the Spirit of God, yet act lower than an animal in their behavior. Now, that is puzzling! That is the work of Satan, because he hates God and everything God loves. He perverts the ways of God, causing men and women to reject God and stumble over truth. Then he goes around accusing us before God. But he is a defeated foe.

> *When I consider Your heavens, the work of Your fingers, the moon and the stars, which You have ordained, what is man that You are mindful of him, and the son of man that You visit him? For You have made him a little lower than the angels, and You have crowned him with glory and honor. You have made him to have dominion over the works of Your hands; You have put all things under his feet,*
>
> Psalms 8:3–6 (NKJV)

> *Then I heard a loud voice shouting across the heavens, "It has happened at last—the salvation and power and kingdom of our God, and the authority of his Christ! For the Accuser has been thrown down to earth—the one who accused our brothers and sisters before our God day and night.*
> Revelation 12:10 (NLT)

You don't see a bear sitting and talking out a business deal with a horse or a hippopotamus having lunch with a zebra. An animal is an animal, and a human is a human. We can talk and reason with other humans from all walks of life. But some human beings make animals look on us with dismay and confusion. Have you ever seen a dog look at a person and tilt his head as if to say, "What in the world are you doing?" God has given human beings a mind that can reason like him, yet some animals act better than humans.

You will never see a male elephant trying to mate with a female bear, not even with another male elephant. You do not see the animal kingdom mating with their same sex gender. But male humans will lie with other male humans, and female humans will lay with other female humans and says what's wrong with that. Some have even said, "God made me this way." That's not true. Satan tricked Eve into believing a lie and she then caused Adam to disobey God. As a result of the fall of our ancestors Adam and Eve, we are born with a sin nature, one that rebels against God, but God never made any of us to commit sin.

God is not a God of perversion and confusion. He is a God of purity and order. The Lord is a God of reproduction and multiplication. Two males in a relationship or two females in a relationship cannot reproduce. Any life form that doesn't reproduce is not of God. This does not include a couple who for some medical reason are not able to have children. Or as we read in the first chapter, the Lord is waiting for an appointed time to give them children. Anyone who believes or acts that way is completely out of order. The Lord hasn't created anyone or anything to act that way. The Lord God Almighty has shown us and told us why people act this way. He said people behave this way because they have rejected him. It's called sin and rebellion. And repentance will correct that and make you right with God.

> *Yes, they knew God, but they wouldn't worship him as God or even give him thanks. And they began to think up foolish ideas of what God was like. The result was that their minds became dark and confused. So God let them go ahead and do whatever shameful things their hearts desired. As a result, they did vile and degrading things with each other's bodies. Instead of believing what they knew was the truth about God they deliberately chose to believe lies. That is why God abandoned them to their shameful desires. Even the women turned against the natural way to have sex and instead indulged in sex with each other. And the men, instead of having normal sexual relationships with women, burned with lust for each other. Men did shameful things with other men and, as a result, suffered within themselves the penalty they so richly deserved. When they refused to acknowledge God, he abandoned them to their evil minds and let them do things that should never be done.*
> Romans 1:21, 24–28 (NLT)

Men for centuries have suppressed the truth. Darwin isn't by himself, nor was he the first to deny that God, is the Creator of all things, nor shall he be the last. Though these were men of great intelligence, and found the answers in many things, what good is that intelligence if it rules out the existence of the God who gave it?

The Lord knows how he made us. It's bad enough to tell a

lie, but to lie and say God did it is a terrible spot to be in. The Lord doesn't want us to be blind or confused. That is why he gave us his Word, the Bible, so we can know the truth when others come along and say things like, "There is no God," and things like, "There is no absolute truth." To say there is no truth is to say there is no God because God is truth. His word is truth and God and his word, are one.

> *The fool hath said in his heart, There is no God. Corrupt are they, and have done abominable iniquity: there is none that doeth good.*
>
> Psalms 53:1 (KJV)

> *A fool has no delight in understanding, but in expressing his own heart.*
>
> Proverbs 18:2 (NKJV)

> *The heart of the prudent acquires knowledge, and the ear of the wise seeks knowledge.*
>
> Proverbs 18:15 (NKJV)

> *Teach the wise, and they will be wiser. Teach the righteous, and they will learn more.*
>
> Proverbs 9:9 (NLT)

Our heavenly father wants us to know him, how he interacts with us, what he has done for us and what is he is going to do. The Lord is our loving heavenly Father, and he wants us to know him and to live forever in his presence.

One day a man named Job questioned God, and God answered. It appeared God was angry with Job. But from the very beginning of the story, God was very pleased with Job, and he gave this testimony about him. He said, "Job was a just and upright man, more so than all the people in the land."

> *Then the Lord asked Satan, "Have you noticed my servant Job? He is the finest man in all the earth—a man of complete integrity. He fears God and will have nothing to do with evil."*
>
> Job 1:8 (NLT)

Twice, Satan accused Job of fearing God only because God blessed him. Satan told the Lord if he removed his hand from Job's life, he would curse him. So God tested Job, allowing Satan to take all his wealth, his family, and his health, but God told Satan not to touch his life.

> *Satan replied to the Lord, "Skin for skin—he blesses you only because you bless him. A man will give up everything he has to save his life. But take away his health, and he will surely curse you to your face!" "All right, do with him as you please," the Lord said to Satan. "But spare his life." So Satan left the Lord's presence, and he struck Job with a terrible case of boils from head to foot.*
>
> Job 2:4–7 (NLT)

After about nine months of suffering, Job questioned God about his situation, but he never cursed God or lost his faith in God. And God answered.

> *Then the Lord answered Job from the whirlwind: "Who is this that questions my wisdom with such ignorant words? Brace yourself, because I have some questions for you, and you must answer them. "Where were you when I laid the foundations of the earth? Tell me, if you know so much.*
>
> Job 38:1–4 (NLT)

However, God did not like the things Job's friends said concerning him and who he was. So, in the end, Job had to pray for his friends, or they were doomed.

> *After the Lord had finished speaking to Job, He said to Eliphaz the Temanite: "I am angry with you and with your two friends, for you have not been right in what you said about me, as my servant Job was. Now take seven young bulls and seven rams and go to my servant Job and offer a burnt offering for yourselves. My servant Job will pray for you, and I will accept his prayer on your behalf. I will not treat you as you deserve, for you have not been right in what you said about me, as my servant Job was."*
>
> Job 42:7–8 (NLT)

Hmm! I wonder if Darwin ever had a conversation like that with God. I doubt it! If Darwin really wanted to know, all he had to do was ask God. God wants to talk with us, and he will talk with us about anything. All we have to do is ask him and then listen and watch for the answers.

The problem is not with God. It's people! Sometimes we are too busy to be still and listen. Sometimes we just aren't sensitive enough to recognize when he speaks. Some people are afraid to talk to the Lord God. They may talk to him from time to time rather casually, but they don't stick around and wait for God to speak back to them. Some are afraid of what he will say. And sometimes people don't want to know. But Job wanted an answer, so he questioned God, and God answered.

Unlike the children of Israel, Job was not afraid. God told the children of Israel he wanted to talk with them. And when they heard his voice, they were so afraid they told Moses, "You talk to God for us." They said if God talked to them they would die. Well, why would they think that? God talked to

Moses and he lived, so why would they think they would die? God wanted to talk to them as he did with Moses.

> *And they said to Moses, "You tell us what God says, and we will listen. But don't let God speak directly to us. If he does, we will die!" "Don't be afraid," Moses said, "for God has come in this way to show you His awesome power. From now on, let your fear of Him keep you from sinning!" As the people stood in the distance, Moses entered into the deep darkness where God was.*
> Exodus 20:19–21 (NLT)

If they had let him, they would not have rebelled as they did. Nor would they have followed the false teaching or worshiped the false gods of the other nations around them, which the Lord God Almighty warned them about through Moses. Just think of it, if God had spoken with them as he did with Moses, they would have feared and obeyed him just as Moses did. When God got Moses' attention with the burning bush that never was consumed, Moses turned to see why it was not being consumed. When God spoke, Moses didn't run away; he came closer and chose to listen. Moses became so intimate with God that God called Moses a friend. One time God took and put Moses up in the cleft of the mountain rocks because he asked the Lord to show him what he looks like.

> *And the LORD replied to Moses, "I will indeed do what you have asked, for you have found favor with me, and you are my friend." Then Moses had one more request. "Please let me see your glorious presence," he said.*
> Exodus 33:17–18 (NLT)

> *But He said, "You cannot see My face; for no man shall see Me, and live." And the LORD said, "Here is a place by Me,*

> *and you shall stand on the rock. So it shall be, while My glory passes by, that I will put you in the cleft of the rock, and will cover you with My hand while I pass by. Then I will take away My hand, and you shall see My back; but My face shall not be seen."*
>
> Exodus 33:20–23 (NKJV)

The Lord God loves us, and he wants us to be intimate with him. The Lord speaks to us through his Word, our thoughts, sometimes even in our dreams, but many times we are not sensitive enough to hear him when he is speaking.

There are a few of you reading this book who probably feel that the things I have being sharing are still not enough to convince you that the God I speak of is the one and only true God. You may say, "I'm a Muslim," or some other religion, and few of you may say, "I'm atheist." Well, I'm not talking religion here. I am certainly not talking foolishly. I'm talking about intimacy with the living God of all creation and God who sees you, hears you, rejoices over you, and hurts with you, and he loves you profusely. He is the living God, and he speaks with us as we speak with him.

> *He will be very gracious to you at the sound of your cry; when He hears it, He will answer you.*
>
> Isaiah 30:19b (NKJV)

> *The Lord, the Maker of the heavens and earth—the Lord is his name—says this: Ask me and I will tell you some remarkable secrets about what is going to happen here.*
>
> Jeremiah 33:3 (NLT)

The Lord God wants intimacy, not religion. Most people, who consider themselves religious, usually don't know the voice of

God. They know religion. Religion is man's way of reaching God. Jesus is God's way of reaching all humanity. I've heard people who, are not, in a relationship with God and his son Jesus, say they religiously pray. When they were through speaking, I asked them, "What did the Lord say?" And each time I did, they had a puzzled look on their face as if to say, "He speaks?" You see, those who practice a religion talk to God, but those of us who have a relationship with God in Christ Jesus talks to God, and he to us. I am not saying God will not speak to people who practice religion, but have no relationship with him, because he will. He has shown us he does in his word many times to get people's attention. The problem is some people won't listen or they do not recognize it is the Lord.

He talks to us through our conscience. Sometimes it's so clear you think you've heard it aloud. Some have claimed they had, but only a few. He speaks to us by the Holy Spirit, from his word, through other people, creation and events. He reveals himself, his desires and his instructions to our minds, even in a dream. Did you know you can hear him when it thunders? Your voice has a sound, why not would God's?

> *"My heart pounds as I think of this. It leaps within me. Listen carefully to the thunder of God's voice as it rolls from his mouth. It rolls across the heavens, and his lightning flashes out in every direction. Then comes the roaring of the thunder— the tremendous voice of his majesty. He does not restrain the thunder when he speaks. God's voice is glorious in the thunder. We cannot comprehend the greatness of his power.*
> Job 37:1–5 (NLT)

If you go through the Bible and read it thoroughly, you will see how the Lord spoke, often before anyone spoke to him.

He would come down in the cool of the day and walk with Adam and Eve. He was so impressed with Enoch he took him back with him. In Noah's day, the people of the earth were corrupted, but the Lord saw that Noah was a righteous man and told him to build an ark, so that he and his family may be saved, because he was going to destroy everything living. Then he made a covenant with Noah, his family, and all the animals after they departed the ark that he would never destroy the earth with a flood again. I believe he did this because it grieved him to see all of creation die like that. And I believe he made this covenant with Noah and all the others so that they would not live in fear that it could happen again to them, having seen what happened to all the others.

The Lord spoke to Abraham and told him to leave his country and go to another land, a place he was going to give him and his descendants forever. Then he promised Abraham an everlasting covenant of eternal life that comes through Jesus, the Christ. Abraham believed God to the point of giving up the life of his promised son, Isaac, born to him and Sarah.

Because of his faith to hear the Lord, believe the Lord, and obey the Lord, Abraham received the biggest blessing of all. The Lord said, "No, Abraham, do not harm your son, but because you were going to do it out of complete obedience to me, I will give up my one and only Son instead. And through your son Isaac I will send my Son to give his life for all humanity. To everyone who believes as you have done they too will receive the same blessings I am giving you. And I will bless those who bless you, and I will curse those who curse you." That's an eternal promise to Abraham and to all who have believed in the Son of God.

Remember, God is a perpetual God. He wasn't only talking about the birth of Isaac, but the seed of Jesus Christ that came through Abraham's seed, Isaac and Jacob (Israel), Boaz and Ruth, down to David and Bathsheba, down to the Holy Spirit and the Virgin Mary, and now unto every born-again person in Christ.

> *Let me put it another way. The law was our guardian and teacher to lead us until Christ came. So now, through faith in Christ, we are made right with God. But now that faith in Christ has come, we no longer need the law as our guardian. So you are all children of God through faith in Christ Jesus. And all who have been united with Christ in baptism have been made like him. There is no longer Jew or Gentile, slave or free, male or female. For you are all Christians—you are one in Christ Jesus. And now that you belong to Christ, you are the true children of Abraham. You are his heirs, and now all the promises God gave to him belong to you.*
> Galatians 3:24–29 (NLT)

When the Lord called Moses to lead the children of Israel out of the bondages of Egypt, Moses didn't go to God and say, "God, send me to Egypt to deliver my people out of bondage." No, the Lord spoke to Moses first. The one thing that turned Moses around into the face of God was when he went to seek the truth of why a bush was burning but not being consumed. This amazed him, and he went to investigate it. Then God spoke to him, and from that moment on, Moses knew who the true and living God was and what the Lord wanted him to do.

When you really want to know the truth about something, you will turn in pursuit of it and without fail, you will learn the truth because God sees you seeking to know it, and he will let nothing stop you from having it.

God knows what is in our hearts. He put desires in us to help us get to a place or a thing he has for us. The Lord set Moses up with that bush. He knew what was in Moses' heart, and he wanted to use it. You see, Moses was raised in Egypt, where they worshiped many gods and idols. So he didn't know the true and living God personally, but he did have a sense that there was a God, that he was good, and that he did not create man to rule over another man, nor beat another man, woman, or child.

Moses was so humble that God called him *friend* and said Moses was the meekest man on earth. God spoke to him face to face. And the Lord got angry with those who opposed Moses or spoke wrongly to him or of him. God judged even Moses' own sister for speaking against Moses. What a testimony to have from the Lord himself. Do you ever wonder what kind of testimony he may have concerning you?

> *And Miriam and Aaron spake against Moses because of the Ethiopian woman whom he had married: for he had married an Ethiopian woman.*
>
> Numbers 12:1 (KJV)

> *With him will I speak mouth to mouth, even apparently, and not in dark speeches; and the similitude of the Lord shall he behold: wherefore then were ye not afraid to speak against my servant Moses? And the anger of the Lord was kindled against them; and he and the cloud departed from off the tabernacle; and, behold, Miriam became leprous, white as snow: and Aaron looked upon Miriam, and, behold, she was leprous.*
>
> Numbers 12:8–10 (KJV)

Now if the Lord would fall upon Moses' sister because she spoke against him, how much more on those who speak directly against the Lord God himself? Now to the few of you who feel this do not apply to you because you say, "I'm an atheist, and I am not a part of any religion." That is not true! Atheism is a religion too.

Some people have a *belief* in God, and a few people have a *belief* that there is no God. Either way, you believe in something. Religion simply means *a systematic belief, altitude, rules, and regulations by which one chooses to live.*

So if you happen to be an atheist and someone says to you, "What religion are you?" To say, "I do not believe in religion or God," you're truthfully saying, "My faith is the religion of unbelief." However, I hope you come to true faith in the Lord Jesus, the Almighty God who made us and loves us all.

> *God showed how much he loved us by sending his only Son into the world so that we might have eternal life through him. This is real love. It is not that we loved God, but that he loved us and sent his Son as a sacrifice to take away our sins.*
> 1 John 4:9–10 (NLT)

I'm sure there are a few of you reading this book who still feel this is not enough to be convinced, but that's okay because that is the job of the Spirit of God, who is also called the Spirit of truth. My job is to spread the good news about having life through God's Son, the Lord Jesus, and the Holy Spirit's place is to convict the world of its sins and to open our understanding, that he may draw us into the true knowledge of who God is. And I know he is doing just that, or you would not be reading this book.

If you do not believe that Jesus is the Son of God because of what your religion teaches or maybe you are an atheist but you have an open mind and heart and you want to know more, there is a wonderful book titled *The Case for a Creator*, written by Lee Strobel, who was once an atheist. Just like the Spirit of God did for the Apostle Paul, C.S. Lewis, Lee Strobel, and many others, he will open any eyes and give clear understanding to anyone who really wants to know truth. If you wish to know more, please check out this Web site for a more in-depth study: *http://www.leestrobel.com*.

The King James Bible would also be a very good place to start. If you happen to be one of those people who feels that the King James Bible has contradictions in it or hard to understand, you can always read another translation, such as the New Living Translation, the New International Version, or the Amplified Bible. If you still have a problem with the translated Bibles, then you can always learn the original languages the scriptures were first written in and read them. Either way, you have no excuse for not knowing. God knows how to deliver his Word. And anyone who tampers with it, he said he would deal with them. Therefore, you can trust and rely on his Word.

> *God will add to him the plagues that are written in this book; and if anyone takes away from the words of the book of this prophecy, God shall take away his part from the Book of Life, from the holy city, and from the things which are written in this book.*
>
> Revelation 22:18–19 (NKJV)

Hopefully I have shared enough that you will at least ask God to reveal to you who he is if you are unsure or do not believe. Better to ask God than to be blindly led by men like Darwin. You still have the chance to know the truth. Those who never believed and have gone on in death no longer have a chance. It's all up to you now. God has always been and always will be. He is the infinite God.

He wrote his own Word first with his own finger in stone on Mount Sinai and gave it to Moses and the children of Israel. Then centuries later, some men decided to put their words of theory in writing on paper—paper that was created from the dust of the earth, which God made—and then says, "God doesn't exist." Either you will believe the truth of God's Word that comes from the very mouth of God himself or be deceived by the words that came from the mouth of men who don't even believe in their own Creator.

> *It is written, Man shall not live by bread alone, but by every word that proceedeth out of the mouth of God.*
> Matthew 4:4b (KJV)

> *God is not a man that He should lie; neither the son of man, that he should repent; hath He said and shall He not do? Or hath He spoken and shall He not make it good?*
> Numbers 23:19 (KJV)

Darwin and a few others like him chose to deny the existence of their Creator. If God didn't exist, Darwin and others like him would not have existed either. God created him through the birth canal of his mother. Now, isn't that something? This man was formed from a seed, grew in the womb of his mother, and then he grew up big and tall and believed he knew it all. Because he offered so much to life, I hope, on his deathbed before he breathed his last breath he believed.

The U.S. National Library of Medicine states: "An important property of DNA is that it can replicate, or make copies of itself. Each strand of DNA in the double helix can serve as a pattern for duplicating the sequence of bases. This is critical when cells divide because each new cell needs to have an exact copy of the DNA present in the old cell." And just as DNA begets DNA, so people beget people, and families beget families, talent begets talents. All of this is passed down to the seed. What's in the father and the mother is passed on to their children. Each child is a replica of the parents and so are gifts and callings. Gifts and calling begets gifts and callings. Queens beget queens and kings beget kings. King David begot King Solomon. King Solomon begot King Jeroboam. King Jeroboam begot King Zechariah, King Zechariah and so forth.

Political Leaders beget Political Leaders. John Adams was the first vice president, serving under George Washington for eight years, and in 1797, he was elected the second president, where he established the Library of Congress and Department of Navy. His son, John Quincy, became the sixth President. Not modern enough?

Former President George Bush Senior was the forty-first president elected of the United States from the period of 1989–1993. He also served as vice president under the late, great former President Ronald Wilson Reagan from the period of 1981–1989. His son, George Bush Junior was the forty-third president of the United States. He was sworn into office on January 20, 2001, re-elected on November 2, 2004, and was sworn in for a second term on January 20, 2005. Prior to his presidency, President Bush Junior also served for six years as the forty-sixth governor of the state of Texas. He and his other brothers followed in their father's footsteps in the arena of law and government.

Other politicians beget politicians. Former Senator Harold Ford Senior groomed his son in the arena of politics and when he left office his son, Harold Ford Junior, was elected to his father's seat in Congress. Law professor and former New York State Senator Basil Patterson, begot law professor David Patterson, who, following in his father's footstep in the arena of law and government, now holds the position as the governor of New York.

Lawyers beget lawyers, for example, attorney Jay Sekulow, his son, attorney Logan Sekulow and his staff of attorneys, are some of the best lawyers in the land. Attorney Jay Sekulow is chief counsel for the ACLJ (American Center for Law and Justice). He specializes in constitutional law. He is also chief counsel of the ECLJ (European Center for Law and Justice). His son Logan Sekulow follows in his father's footsteps. Not only is his son a lawyer, they both host a radio and Television broadcast "Jay Sekulow Live," is aired on over eight hundred TV and radio stations. His son Logan host "The Logan Show."

Business owners beget business owners, for example, the Sam Walton family. Shoemakers beget shoemakers, carpenters beget carpenters, and etc. Jesus followed in the footsteps of his earthly stepfather Joseph, who was a carpenter. Jesus in his earthly ministry also followed the will of our heavenly Father. He said several times, "I always do what I see the father do."

> *Jesus replied, "I assure you, the Son can do nothing by himself. He does only what he sees the Father doing. Whatever the Father does, the Son also does.*
> *John 5:19 (NLT)*

Pastors beget pastors. Dr. Billy Graham's, one of the world's greatest pastor, son, Franklin Graham, followed in his footsteps. Joel Osteen Senior founded one of the world's largest ministries—Lakewood Church. Its humble beginning started in a converted feed store on the outskirts of Houston. Now the church consists of more than twenty thousand members. Pastor Osteen Sr. passed away in 1999, and now, his youngest son, Joel Osteen Junior, pastors it, and his other sons work alongside him as well. People beget people, and gifts and talents of parents beget gifts and talents to their children. If you don't know what gifts and talents the Lord has imparted to you, just look back a generation or two. It's not that hard to recognize. If that doesn't work, you can always do the best thing, ask God to show you.

Africans beget Africans. Caucasians beget Caucasians. Mexicans beget Mexicans. Italians beget Italians, and so forth. The color of skin, hair, body shape, and even blood types are developed all after its kind. Have you ever seen two Chinese parents reproduce Mexican children? Or two African parents reproduce Caucasian children? Certainly not! They can only reproduce after their own kind and in their own likeness. Even mixed parents reproduce mixed children because the genes were mixed.

Every nationality produces after its kind, and so does the gifts and callings in them. Every generation produces after its kind. They inherit their wisdom, their knowledge, their ignorance, their wealth, their poverty, their talents, their businesses, their health, their diseases, their behavior patterns, and all. But many have lost sight of this, and many others do not know this. Surely, this helps to make things a lot clearer that God has made everything to reproduce after its own kind or likeness.

Isn't it strange how people go to great lengths to find out the history of their ancestors, but rarely pursue it to find out what their ancestors' gifts and callings were and how they connect with their own? That would help them find their places in life as well. Not only are our names, DNA, and properties or estates, mental and emotional environments passed down from generation to generation, but more importantly, what many forget is that the gifts and vocations are passed down also. God is a God of purpose. He has designed us to seek knowledge and witty inventions. We are designed to create just like our Creator. Therefore, since he created us, he has a purpose for us, and since he has a purpose for us, he has a job for us to do, and since he has a job for us to do, it behooves us to get the plan from the one who has it. We need the Lord and his divine guidance to lead and help us fulfill our purpose and that of our nation. We need to turn back to the God of the Bible; the God of our fathers, Abraham Isaac and Jacob.

It is no coincidence that many of our nation's past and present leaders are descendants of Abraham. It is no coincidence that land of the USA is laid out just like the Tabernacle and the Holy of Holies, which Moses and the children of Israel built, as instructed by the Lord. It is no coincidence that the property there in Washington D.C. where our leaders gather, is laid out in the exact same pattern of the tabernacle and the temple of Solomon before it was destroyed. It is no coincidence that the entire land of the United States' resources is positioned state to state, in the same order as the Tabernacle and the Holy of Holies. Everything is identical. Evangelist Perry Stone has done a magnificent study revealing this. You can order the entire study at www.voe.org.

It is no coincidence that the USA and Britain sides with Israel. Studies show these two nations are the lost tribes of Israel, Manasseh and Ephraim, the sons of Joseph whom Isaac blessed before his death.

> *Joseph took the boys from their grandfather's knees, and he bowed low to him. Then he positioned the boys so Ephraim was at Jacob's left hand and Manasseh was at his right hand. But Jacob crossed his arms as he reached out to lay his hands on the boys' heads. So his right hand was on the head of Ephraim, the younger boy, and his left hand was on the head of Manasseh, the older. Then he blessed Joseph and said, "May God, the God before whom my grandfather Abraham and my father, Isaac, walked, the God who has been my shepherd all my life, and the angel who has kept me from all harm—may he bless these boys. May they preserve my name*

and the names of my grandfather Abraham and my father, Isaac. And may they become a mighty nation."
Genesis 48:12–16 (NLT)

It is no coincidence that Senator Joe Lieberman stood before an audience of people attending the Christians United for Israel Summit and said *"I am your brother Joseph."* It is no coincidence that the USA sits right in the middle of the word Jerusalem (JER-USA-LEM), the very city and heart of God. America has been called and appointed by the God of our fathers long ago, to be a Holy Nation, but like the children of Israel did, many in the body of the Lord Jesus Christ in America have gone after other gods and have embraced them. Many embrace the word of everyone else, but we are failing to embrace and uphold the word of our God and Savoir.

The Lord himself established this land to be a God fearing nation. A Christian nation! But we have an enemy called Satan, who is trying hard to hi-jack the land and overthrow the will of God; just like he tried in the heavens, but got kicked out; just like he did when he tricked Eve to get Adam to rebel against God and caused them to be put out of their own land; just like he did the children of Israel when they rebelled against God and was taken from their own land into captivity. And he has caused the people of the United States of America to rebel against God, so we too may lose our authority, rights and privileges in this land. But he forgot something, God is in charge and no one and nothing can overthrow the will of God.

You can make many plans, but the LORD's purpose will prevail.
Proverbs 19:21 (NLT)

I believe this nation is destined to be one Holy Nation of people from all walks of life under one God. A people who believes and worship the name of the only true and living God and his son, the Lord Jesus Christ. Some people were forced here against their own will, but I believe the Lord said; *I can still use that to fulfill my purpose!* Some snuck in, risking their living and that of their children, but I believe the Lord said, *I can still use that too to fulfill my purpose!* Our heavenly father has always had a plan for America. My hope and prayer is that our leaders will once again know the vision God has for this nation. And I pray that the Lord will finish what he started with our nation, so America the Great, will not become America the Late.

Life, Liberty and Lucre

A party gives laughter, and wine gives happiness, and money gives everything!

Ecclesiastes 10:19 (NLT)

I love to travel, and one of my main methods for doing so is by cruise ship. I first determine to go. Then I select a destination and an appointed time and even the length of time I will travel. Then I let my vacation run its course. Before I know it, the time has come and gone, and it's all over! "Home again, home again, jiggety-jig!"

Many of you have planned family vacations, usually by picking out a destination. Then you make all the necessary travel plans, and then you begin telling everybody you are going away, where you are traveling, and even making a list of some of the things you plan to do. Then as the departure time draws near, you began running around like a chicken with its head cut off, shopping and preparing those last-minute things that need to be done before leaving and things needed for the vacation.

Then you finish packing the family bags, and the time comes to pack the family car. You back out of the garage and you take off! Okay, everyone is happy and excited.

Sometimes you encounter some problems along the way, and other times things go as planned. Then, when it's all over, you return home and back into the garage where you started. It's all over. Hurrah! You're home again! All to put your nose back to the grindstone.

As troubling as the airline industry may be, millions still travel the friendly skies. For some, the takeoff is exciting. For others it's the landing, while others are shaking in their boots. As for me, I love them both.

The airplane takes off from the ground, runs it course from destination to destination, and then it returns to the same ground it left. So it is with life. From the dust of the ground we have come, and from the dust of the ground we shall return, but our spirit (the breath of God) goes back to the Lord. That's life!

Sadly enough, though a plane was scheduled to arrive at an appointed time, sometimes it never makes it, due to a malfunction, an act of nature, or a criminal act. So it is with some who never get the glorious opportunity to see life or finish experiencing life. Life is so short here on earth. It comes, and then it goes. King Solomon puts it this way:

> *For then the dust will return to the earth, and the spirit will return to God who gave it.*
> *Ecclesiastes 12:7 (NLT)*

> *Generations come and go but nothing really changes.*
> *Ecclesiastes 1:4 (NLT)*

And James, a brother of the Lord, said:

> *For what is your life? It is a vapour that appeareth for a little time and then vanished away.*
>
> James 4:14 (KJV)

Now that's short! We certainly don't have a lot of time to wait, if we are planning to finish our course successfully. We've got to know what our part is and complete it. We need the Lord and we cannot afford to live life apart from his word. To do this is to waste not only our own lives but also the lives of our children. In fact, the Lord said it's the lack of knowledge that causes us to perish.

> *My people are being destroyed because they don't know me.*
>
> Hosea 4:6a (NLT)

Many of our leaders are the blame for causing people to be destroyed. Whether the leaders of a church, a family, a city, a firm, or leaders of the nations. When the Lord addressed an issue, he addresses the husband, a leader of a city or of the nation. The decisions they make affect us all. Any time you see much disorder and chaos in a nation, it is because someone is rebelling against the word of God. That's why it is important to choose leaders who revere the Lord God, and continually seek his wisdom and guidance for the nation or whatever position of leadership he or she is appointed to oversee.

One of the greatest kings that ever ruled was King David. He was not only the king, but he was a mighty warrior, who fought alongside the toughest warriors in his army. These warriors were descendants of Gad, one of the sons of Jacob (Israel).

King David sought God's counsel many times, even concerning wars, and God told King David exactly what to do.

> *But after a while the Philistines returned and again spread out across the valley of Rephaim. And once again David asked the Lord what to do. "Do not attack them straight on," the* Lord *replied. "Instead, circle around behind them and attack them near the balsam trees. When you hear a sound like marching feet in the tops of the balsam trees, attack! That will be the signal that the* Lord *is moving ahead of you to strike down the Philistines." So David did what the Lord commanded, and he struck down the Philistines all the way from Gibeon to Gezer.*
>
> 2 Samuel 5:22–25 (NLT)

> *Some Gadites joined David at the stronghold in the wilderness, mighty men of valor, men trained for battle, who could handle shield and spear, whose faces were like the faces of lions, and were as swift as gazelles on the mountains:*
>
> 1 Chronicles 12:8–9 (NKJV)

> *Gad, a troop shall overcome him: but he shall overcome at the last.*
>
> Genesis 49:19 (KJV)

David also sought the Lord another time concerning their enemies. The Amalekites came into their city on a day when David and his men were away. When they returned, they found their city burned and all the women and children taken captive. David's men cried with much anguish and anger, because they loved their families. They were so overcome with grief they wanted to kill David. David cried to the Lord and asked should they go after them. The Lord said yes and recover all.

> *Now David was greatly distressed, for the people spoke of stoning him, because the soul of all the people was grieved, every man for his sons and his daughters. But David strengthened himself in the LORD his God. Then David said to Abiathar the priest, Ahimelech's son, "Please bring the ephod here to me." And Abiathar brought the ephod to David. So David inquired of the LORD, saying, "Shall I pursue this troop? Shall I overtake them?" And He answered him, "Pursue, for you shall surely overtake them and without fail recover all."*
>
> 1 Samuel 30:6–8 (NKJV)

As you can see, when leaders of the nations ask the Lord for direction, he gives it and gives victory over their enemies. The Lord himself has and still will fight a nation at war with their enemies. Several times in the scriptures he fought against Israel's enemies himself.

I was grieved and shocked to see the media and some of our political leaders run down Former President George Bush, Jr. and our U.S. Armed Forces, in mist of a war. And right in front of our nation's enemies. I mean I was shocked. I thought how could they? Here we sit in our quiet homes and fine restaurants, while these brave men and women were risking their life being shot at or blown up by a bomb, fighting our enemies. In times of war, we should get behind our leaders and armed forces no matter our differences with support and prayer. We should ask God to reveal to them his will, a strategic plan to win, his protection over them and his rebuke if needed. When they are safely back home then let's deal with those differences. Whatever has to be dealt with in the mist of the war, do it, but not in front of the enemies. The Democrats constantly argued with Republicans on how they plan to win the war. You don't openly tell your strategies for defeating your enemy. Talk about a nut case. Did anybody else see this?

Many of us have no excuse when it comes to getting knowledge of God and secular knowledge because this knowledge is all around us, and the Internet has made it easier to access. For years, many of us have heard these words: "What you don't know can't hurt you!" That very statement contradicts the Word of God. What you don't know will destroy you.

The Lord God wants our children, as well as us, to be well educated and full of his wisdom. Yet we have an educational system failing to turn out wise and knowledgeable students because they continue to reject the Word of God concerning the principles of true wisdom and knowledge for life and have embraced fallacies and folly. So have some of the leaders in the church. However, in order to weed out the bad leaders and pastors, the Lord said he would give us leaders according to his heart.

> *And I will give you leaders after my own heart, who will guide you with knowledge and understanding.*
> Jeremiah 3:15 (NLT)

God wants us to turn to him, and that is the starting point of a new and better life. It's up to you to ask the Lord to show you that kind of pastor and it is up to you to read the Word of God and teach it to your children and let him show you what is your purpose and place in this life and the lives of your children.

The Lord has preset life, things, and time in the earth. He did this from the beginning of the heavens above to the earth beneath, from the land, ocean, and seas, from the plants to the trees, and from the insects to mankind. The Lord also has an appointed position for everyone and an appointed time for everything. Everything has been preset except the will of man. God made us free will agents. However, we become set in our ways through habits and the influence of other things or people in our environment. It is evidently clear in creation and the lives that have gone on before us that we all have a purpose for being here. But it is God's final destiny after we fulfill our destiny here on earth to spend eternity with him.

We all have a pre-planned destiny, but because of the lack of knowing and acknowledging God, many never come to know their purpose and destiny. One of the most brilliant men of God, Dr. Myles Munroe, said, "The graveyard is full of unfulfilled purpose," meaning that millions have died and never fulfilled their purpose. He stated that it was the richest place on earth because it was full of ideas, dreams, inventions, books, masterpieces, businesses, and ministries. There are many reasons for this. Sometimes it's because of pride, greed, envy, and oppression on the part of an individual and sometimes as a result of treatment from others; Sometimes it is just plain ole' laziness. But the main reason is that people never realize they have been given a purpose in life specifically from God.

Some people learn their life's destiny from the womb. Jesus knew his purpose, and Mary, his mother, and his earthly father, Joseph, knew Jesus' purpose before he was born. We've covered this more in, *"Knowing Your Child's Destiny before Birth."* Some people have learned their destiny, and they fulfill it to the utmost. Some have learned it, but they get off course. Others never knew there was a course. Thank God we don't have to be in darkness concerning our life's purpose or other people and things. The more time we give to getting knowledge and the more we continue to spend time with the Lord, the more he increases us and brings us to our full destiny.

Our purpose in life was never intended to be a secret, but revealed. The Lord is not trying to keep us hidden from the world. He sent us to serve and represent him in the world. The Lord wants us to know our gifts and purpose. He reveals the end of it to us in our spirit, in his Word, sometimes through a word of prophecy, and sometimes in dreams. Then he confirms it over and over through our gifts, the words of others, and again sometimes in our dreams. He reveals to us the knowledge and wisdom we need to attain his promises and he helps us in carrying out our purpose. Above all things, God's Word is an absolute and sure Word concerning any matter of life. Before you make your final decision, be sure it is in line with the word. If it does, you'll have peace concerning it.

> *Ask, and it shall be given you; seek and ye shall find; knock, and it shall be opened unto you: For every one that asketh receiveth; he that seeketh findeth; to him that knocketh it shall be opened.*
>
> Matthew 7:7–8 (KJV)

So I did. I asked! *Lord, please help me to better understand life; people; money and relationships. Help me to see things and life from your point of view. Why are so many families, relationships, and children's lives being destroyed and so out of order?*

The Lord said this is the problem: *People seek money, relationships, and sexual gratification before pursuing and developing their gifts and callings I have given them.*

Because of this, many lives are out of order, and many families are in total chaos. People have no sense of who they are, or why they're here, nor do they know concerning their children, so they wander through life being destructive instead of productive. When people marry, many times they don't marry with a purpose or a vision. Instead, they marry for sex or for money. Therefore, they don't marry people who share their gifts and calling. I have heard this statement many times and found it to be very true. "When you don't know the purpose of a person or a thing, abuse is inevitable!"

After talking with the Lord about this, I sought all the more! I began reading more of the Scriptures and other books, along with lessons learned from my pastor. And viola! More of God's wisdom and knowledge began to flow. As I continued to pray and read, more and more was revealed to me, and I saw and understood things in the Scriptures I had not seen before, even in the lives of people around me every day, especially those who were married and had children.

Some of them were married to the people who shared their same gifts, and even their children had the same or similar gifts and interests. Then there were parents who had gifts that were totally opposite of each other and the children had no idea who they were or what their calling was. Then there was the unmarried parent in the same condition, only many of these parents, namely the fathers, had no idea where their children were, and many didn't even care. Their children too are lost to wander around in life with no purpose or a sense of direction.

Teach your children to choose the right path, and when they are older, they will remain upon it.
Proverbs 22:6 (NLT)

Parents are commanded to direct their children, and how can they know which way to go if we are not directing them? And how can you teach them if you don't know which way they are to go? The only way to know is to get the directions and instruction from the one who created us and our purpose. The descendants of Abraham increased in wealth far greater because of their father's knowledge and obedience to God. The Lord himself stated it was due to this that he knew he could bless Abraham.

> *I have singled him out so that he will direct his sons and their families to keep the way of the* Lord *and do what is right and just. Then I will do for him all that I have promised."*
> Genesis 18:19 (NLT)

Knowing one's gifts and life's purpose is very important to one's future and relationships especially those with children, yet many do not know this. Marriage has a purpose, and when the purpose is not known, abuse is inevitable. That's why there are so many divorces, affairs, broken homes, broken relationships and broken lives.

Relationships will not work if you don't take the time to know first of all who you are as an individual and your purpose. Then get to know others by learning and understand their ways and purpose for life. The lack of knowing a person and that person's purpose is one of the main reasons that many relationships such as marriages fail.

God commands the husband—not the wife but the husband—to dwell with his wife according to knowledge. What knowledge? The knowledge concerning one's wife; her purpose, her gifts, and how she thinks, feels, reacts, and her likes and dislikes. In other words, watch her closely, studying her ways. What makes her tick, in other words! The husband who understands this watches her closely. He knows what makes his woman ticks. When you do this, you can get a lot from God and her.

In order to do this, he must have a personal relationship with the Lord God and patterning after him according to his word. Then he can successfully fulfill his role in life, his role as a husband and the training of his children.

> *In the same way, you husbands must give honor to your wives. Treat her with understanding as you live together. She may be weaker than you are, but she is your equal partner in God's gift of new life. If you don't treat her as you should, your prayers will not be heard.*
> I Peter 3:7 (NLT)

I have always desired a godly husband, but here in the last few years, I have desired in more detail—one with whom I can work and share a business, working side by side together each day and working together in the kingdom of God as well. Someone with whom we share the same moral values, vision, gifts, ministry calling, and someone who definitely loves the Lord and has committed to live by his standards and not the standards of this world; A husband who understands his role as husband, provider, protector and priestly leadership in the home; One who will be as loyal to me as I will be to him. This is a hot little topic written about in my 3rd book, *"Who Can Find A Faithful Man."* In this book I share in great details the purpose of a calling, a mate, and how they all relate to one another. Be sure you stay on the lookout for this one.

My desire and prayer is that I too would make the man I so greatly desire a wonderful wife whom I complement and I know I will greatly enhance his life. But the more unfaithfulness I saw, the more it seems impossible, but I still have a little faith left.

And the more my desire increased for a faithful man, so did the grief, because the more you learn to be right and not see it, the more it grieves you.

> *For in much wisdom is much grief, And he who increases knowledge increases sorrow.*
>   Ecclesiates 1:18 (NKJV)

We all have gifts that fit the call of a mate or a particular ministry vocation. However, I learned this late in life, rather than during my younger years, that when you have a desire to marry, the main things you should look for in a mate are common goals and desires, gifts and vocation, and more importantly, biblical beliefs and moral values.

It's God's idea and design for families to work together and pass down the family visions and trades. God is a perpetual God and a generational God. I have prayed and ask the Lord to bless me with a spouse that I complement and one whom we share the same visions and values for life and even the same or similar gifts and talent. I'm still hoping and believing. If that is your desire too, don't give up. Keep believing and keep preparing. In fact, it would be very wise to be sure marriage is God's will for you and that marriage is something you really want.

When God brings the two of you together, then you can increase and multiply together as one mind and heart. When you acknowledge God concerning the affairs of your life, he will answer you because he wants you to fulfill your life's destiny together or as a single person. God is not a wasteful God. He sent us here with a purpose, and he wants it carried out. Little by little, you will begin to see it unfolding and the pieces of your life coming together, as you spend time with him in prayer, bible study and as you continue to flow in the gifts he has given you. When impatience or hopelessness tries to creep in, ask the Lord to help you to be patience until that season of your life comes into full bloom. That's goes for me too, just as much as you. And as for patience having her perfect work, I have a long way to go.

There is a time for everything, a season for every activity under heaven.
          Ecclesiastes 3:1 (NLT)

God is a God of order. In other words, first things first! God has placed gifts and callings in the parents, and these same gifts and callings are passed down to their children. Why, because each generation needs those same gifts and callings. Every generation needs the same services in order to function. Every generation needs pastors, teachers, doctors, judges, lawyers, bankers, scientists, food services, tailors, shoemakers, construction workers, transportation, electricians, armed forces, writers, journalists, etc. So God gives these gifts and callings, and he has placed them in every group of people of every nationality, and they are passed down through the seed in order to serve each generation.

Many times, we say things like, "He looks just like his father, and he walks like him too." Or we'll say, "She acts just like her mother; she even talks like her." We know they have the same DNA, body features, and gestures, but we fail to realize that the skills and spiritual gifts are passed down to the seed as well. Some families know this, but there are far too many others who have no idea.

The order of mankind in pursuit of purpose; is to know God first, then the call, and then fulfill it. Usually the gifts and calling you began to display in your childhood years.

As a child, I loved drawing and sewing doll clothes. Though my grandmother sewed and my mother took sewing classes, I did not learn from them. It all seemed to have come naturally as I would spend time alone drawing and cutting up my mother's pillow case to create my little sewing pieces. Yes, the gifts are definitely passed down to the seeds. One of my sisters was a beautician for years, but now she in banking, but her daughter has her gift and create hair styles unlike you ever seen and two of her sons are now barbers.

My mother took notice of my sewing, and she supported and supplied me with the things I needed as I acted them out. She also did this for my siblings as well. One of my sisters started taking piano lessons when she was nine. She graduated with a degree in music from Memphis State University, now called the University of Memphis and now she teaches for the Memphis City Schools and play the piano for the Lord at her church.

I began taking sewing classes in the eighth grade. By the time I entered the tenth grade, I had built up a little clientele in my home, sewing and doing alterations. I started an alteration service in my home, but at that time I had no idea I would own my own alteration and tailoring shop later. I even spoke as if I had a business. I don't remember this, but my mother said I told her one day as I was working, "Momma, my business is picking up!"

I can still remember the day my mother brought me my first sewing machine, I was so happy. It was one of the best days of my life. I also remember how one day I was moving the sewing machine from the table and one side of the case wasn't locked properly, so I dropped it on the floor, breaking the hand wheel. I was afraid to tell my mother, because I thought she would be upset, but I knew I needed it. When I told her, all I can remember is she got it fixed after a few days and I was back in business. Just telling you about this makes me cry, because I can still see just how much my mother loves me.

Today, I have a very successful and affluent alteration and tailoring business, which was established in September of 1987. And I would like to add that my customers are the best customers in the world. Not only do I enjoy sewing for them, they make me feel greatly appreciated and needed. It is a blessing when people tell you they thank God for you. Those are some of the sweetest words one could ever hear. One of my customers, Mrs. Billy Blair, recently went home to be with the Lord. I met her through Talbot's Store around the year of 1988, where I received hundreds of customers. And though she had her health and strength, got around well, even lived just around the corner from the shop, she has never been to my shop. She always wanted me to come to her home. I asked her to come to the shop several times, but she would always say, "*Oh honey, I need you to come here. Can't you come here? I have a lot of things for you to alter. I need you!*" And I would go. And strange as it may seem, sometimes she really had nothing for me to do. We would talk a few minutes and sometimes I would pray. Sometimes, she would speak of her family whom I could tell she loved and missed them. She would offer me something to drink and eat as usual and then I would be on my way.

My family and friends though they never met her, knew of her, because I always spoke of her. I would repeat to them what she would say to me. She will ask me to alter something for her and I would say, "But Mrs. Blair, I don't think that's going to look right." And she always replied saying, "*Oh you can do it! You can do anything!*" And I always did it. I know without a shallow of doubt, the Lord brought her into my life. Thanks Mrs. Blair. I miss you and I love you!

> *Kind words are like honey—sweet to the soul and healthy for the body.*
> Proverbs 16:24 (NLT)

Once you know your gifts or callings, you begin to develop and polish them through school, college, or other forms of studies and in the fields where you work. While in pursuit of your calling or career, you meet someone along the way who shares the same or similar interests, studies, and values. Sometimes you encounter some problems and disagreements along the way, but you work them out or move on until the one who complements you comes along. When you realize that is the person you want to spend the rest of your life with, you begin making stronger commitments to each other. Then you begin to pursue a future together by making goals toward building a life together. After marriage, you begin to increase by having children, and then you begin to multiply through them. In other words, no gifts increase until you multiply them. And you increase and multiply those gifts through your children.

You cannot increase if you are not aware of what the gifts and callings are among your family. And you certainly can't increase when the family is separated or lost in society. That is where a lot of people are, lost in society, especially the youth generation. Many of them have no sense of purpose and direction because the ones who brought them here have left them to roam this earth alone. Alone, you can accomplish little or nothing, but together you have the power to increase and multiply.

> *And the Lord said, Behold they are one people and they all have one language; and this is only the beginning of what they will do, and now nothing they have imagined they can do will be impossible to them.*
> Genesis 11:6 (AMP)

Even for you to be successful in business you need other people in order to succeed and increase. How many times have we heard this statement? "No man is an island." If you try to be, it will not be long before you dry up and die, and so will your dreams and all you strive to achieve.

For nine years, I ran and operated my business mostly alone. I didn't think I could afford to hire anyone. Oh boy was I ever wrong! Nor did I have a sister, brother, or children with sewing skills to help me. I worked very long hours, day and night, to get all the work done. I could never seem to get it all done because the better you use and develop your gift, the more the work will increase. That is the result of God blessing the works of one's hands when doing a good job.

> *Whatever your hand finds to do, do it with your might*
> Ecclesiastes 9:10a (NKJV)

Finally, I was at a point where the more work that came in, the less I could do because I was spending so much time fitting and writing up orders as they came in and handling those that were being picked up. The less I could do the less money I could make. I started coming in very early in the morning and sewing all through the night. On top of that, I was doing the bookkeeping and running all the errands for the needs of the business and my home. There were many nights where I didn't even sleep.

Having so much to do and no one to help, many times I was so stressed out and unable to meet the work's deadline. And we all know what that means. No work done, no money! Yet the bills keep rolling in. Finally, I was forced to get help, and when I did, the business began to multiply, and so did the money. I was able to work less and earn more. Now we have happier customers, employees are happy, and so am I. I had to learn this the hard way. Nobody told me!

> *Here is one alone—no one with him; he neither has a child nor brother. Yet there is no end to all his labor, neither is his eye satisfied with riches, neither does he ask, For whom do labor and deprive myself of good? This is also vanity (emptiness, falsity, and futility); yes, it is a painful effort and unhappy business. Two are better then one, because they have a good (more satisfying) reward for their labor; For if they fall, the one will lift up his fellow. But woe to him who is alone when he falls and has not another to lift him up! Again, if two lie down together, then they have warmth; but how can he be warm alone? And though a man might prevail against him who is alone, two will withstand him, a threefold cord is not quickly broken.*
>
> Ecclesiastes 4:8–12 (AMP)

Not only do our lives have a destiny, but so do our money. It takes money to live and to fulfill a vision. I've often heard people say, "People come and people go!" Well so do money. But where has it gone? Where is it going now? And how do I get it to turn around? Now I know the best investment we can make is in the Kingdom of God. That I have no doubt! But there are other investments to be made that can increase wealth and the more wealth you have, the more you can support the Kingdom of God, your family and anyone else in need.

From elementary to high school, educators taught us lots of knowledge in several subjects and many trades, but they failed to teach us the knowledge of building wealth. The school systems failed to incorporate as part of every school's curriculum money management and investment courses to teach us to exercise the muscles of the mind so we could build wealth, as well as build careers.

Courses like these would keep one from wearing out the muscles of the body that are many times due to being overworked and stressed out from trying to make more money to pay the debts. Being overworked causes you to diminish your health quickly, lose time from family, and keep you from enjoying life along the way.

Financial literacy is absolutely necessary for the growth of a family, a business, a city, a country, etc. Many of our cities and states are suffering for lack of funds because many of these states' and cities' leaders who are making these decisions on how the money should be used are unable to successfully budget these funds. That's because some of the same individuals went through the same school system that taught us nothing about financial literacy.

The school systems should teach investment techniques that show students how to take a part of their earning from their trades and talents and increase and multiply their earning through interest saving, mutual funds, stock investments, a business, real estate investments, etc.

I remember learning how to count money in elementary school using math problems in our math books, and I remember learning how to reconcile a checkbook in my high school economics class, and that class was only recommended as a one-time, half-semester course. But there was nothing about how to build wealth through savings and investments in stocks and mutual funds, etc. There were no classes teaching how to invest and make money work for me. They taught a trade and much knowledge in math, history, science, and several other courses, but nothing on how to master the money made from your trade.

Why not? It's because "we the people" have been the products and the consumers of corruption. If you never read another book, I pray you will, with critical urgency, read *The Marketing of Evil*, by David Kupelian. You will never ever be the same because your eyes will see this nation like never before. No one will ever be able to pull the wool over your eyes again. Ever!

We deal with money every day, and money management classes, technique, and investment courses should be a mandatory part of every school curriculum from elementary and up. If elementary kids can be taught how to put a condom on a banana in health classes, they definitely can be taught how to put money on a stock in the stock market. They can definitely be taught what money is, how it is made, how it relates to one's life, and how to make it grow and multiply.

Now that I have made it near the hill, it seems too late. Nevertheless, I tune into the stock market to learn what I can. I watch the CNBC (Consumer News and Business Channel). I have my computer homepage set to Marketwatch.com. I also listen to Jim Cramer, a former hedge fund manager for Goldman and Sachs. He now hosts his own show, "Mad Money," teaching millions how to trade in the stock market on CNBC. What if shows like this existed years ago?

Jim Cramer said this: *Never take your child to the bank and open up a checking account. Instead open up a brokerage account. Then buy them stocks in McDonald's, and your kids will get excited, and they will learn a lot about the market while they make money.* What if we had been taught this when we were children! Jim Cramer is an excellent teacher. He makes learning the stock market incredibly fun to learn, and he even has small kids watch his show. I wish we had more financial teachers like him who would teach people how to increase the wise and common sense way.

The wise person makes learning a joy; fools spout only foolishness.

Proverbs 15:2 (NLT)

Do you know McDonald's (MCD) went public, trading around $22.00 per share in 1965? Then during the summer of 2003 it dropped to around $12.00 then climbed to $67.00 per share, spring of 2008. It closed out at $57.46, July 14, 2009. I don't think any of us would complain about those profits had we known how and when to buy in and out. And learning when to buy low and sell high as stocks go up and down, increase your profits more. Just think of how much we have bought in to their burgers, happy meals, and coffee every day. Many of us gained from that. We gained a lot of weight.

I like Cramer's advice, but the only problem is that for many of us today, (MCD) stock is too high to buy enough shares to really see a profit, especially now that it has hit peak highs. Nevertheless, it can be done and you can always put your money there if you want, because as long as kids and adults love McDonald's, and real estate market do well, they won't be going anywhere.

MasterCard went public in May of 2006, stock trading around $33.00 per share. By May of 2008, it climbed to $320.00 dollars per share. What a wonderful profit we could have gained, had we been taught or our parents about the wisdom and power of investing. Yes, I bought in, but due to my other obligations and the stock being more than I could afford, I could only buy a few, so my profit was minimum. Nevertheless, I did make a profit.

I can just hear the naysayers saying, *yeah, but look how much they lost. They fell from $320.00 to $180.00.* True, but if you invested at $33.00 per share when it first went public, you would still have a profit of $147.00 per share—a tremendous gain that is still worst singing and dancing about. Visa saw the tremendous response and returns on Master Card and they went public just months later. Though the profits were not as great, there were still profits made.

Can you imagine how many Credit Card Holders have paid compounded interest on MasterCard and Visa's month after month for years but missed the opportunity to gain it all back and with huge profits? Had they known about MasterCard (MA) going public and when to buy, they could have recovered all. That goes for me too! If you could have bought 500 shares of (MA) at 33.00 ($16,500.00) in 2006, those same shares would be worth $320.00 per share. That's $160,000.00 by 2008, just two years later. That's enough money to pay off my house, every single debt I owe, some shopping and vacation, and a little investment money left over to reinvest.

Bank of America (BAC) stock dropped to around $2.30 per share in March of 2009 and climbed to $17.50 by August 20th. If you had brought 5,000 shares at $2.30 per share, totaling $11,500.00, today your shares would be worth $87,500.00. In a 6 month period!

Ford (F) fell to around $1.50 per share in March of 2009 and climb to nearly $8.00 per share by August 21st. Had you brought 10,000 shares at $1.50 per share, totaling $15,000.00 in 6 months you would have $80,000.00.

100 shares of Ford (F) at $1.50 per share would have been a small investment of $150.00, the cost of a pair of designer tennis shoes. 6 months later that small investment would be worth $800.00. Now don't tell me we can't get some kids all fired up about that. If we did, we would get a lot them off the streets from selling drugs.

Children don't want to commit crimes on the streets, they want to live well and have nice things to enjoy in life too. They are not born to commit crimes. They are taught to do it. Many of them do not see a better way of life happening for them, because they are being robbed of their fathers, a good education, their financial future and their peace of mind. Children need mentoring in all areas of life, especially when it comes to wealth. We all need it when it comes to life, love and Lord.

Oh by the way, while the media had everybody all uptight about the AIG (American International Group) ordeal and the government bailing them out with our tax dollars, they were repositioning themselves to skyrocket. In the summer of 2007, AIG stocks priced around $1,500.00 per share. It fell to around $750.00 a share in the summer of 2008. By spring of 2009 AIG shares were around $2.00. Around June 2009 AIG did a 1 for 20 reverse stock split and stock priced somewhere around $14.00 per share. By July 1st it opened at $19.65 fell again to around $13.50 per share and climbed to $50.04 on August 28, 2009. That's great, but I wonder, when the American's tax payers will get their share. Yes, I own a few shares in my portfolio. I hope it reaches the $1,500.00 mark again. Now that the housing market has bottom and moving upward again, it is certainly possible. In the meantime, this is the verse that came to mind concerning future wealth.

> *A good man leaves an inheritance to his children's children,*
> *But the wealth of the sinner is stored up for the righteous.*
> Proverbs 13:22 (NKJV)

God is letting those who are experts at increasing wealth, do it. When he is ready for it, the wicked has to give it up. When that happens, there's going to be the biggest bailout move in all of history.

Now just think, what if we had only a few opportunities like these I just mention years ago? Millions would not have to rely on the government to survive, nor could they control our financial future. But the problem was, and still is, our schools don't teach investing for your future, so children can better position their financial future. If you don't have someone in your life to teach you, you and your children are destined to struggle financially all through life, unless you start making some changes today. Liberate yourself from the limitations placed on you and your children's financial future.

And remember not to let riches become the center of your life.

> *Don't try to get rich by extortion or robbery. And if your wealth increases, don't make it the center of your life.*
> Psalm 62:10(NLT)

I used to hear growing up this saying a whole lot: *Money don't grow on trees!* And they were absolutely right. Money *doesn't* grow on trees. But it certainly does grow in the stock market. You can sit in front of a computer and watch it move up and down from open to close. If only they knew that, then they could have said, *Money don't grow on trees, but let me show you where it does grow!*

Another old wise saying I used to hear a lot as a child was: *If you can't beat 'em! Join 'em!* But they never said how. In other words, if you can't compete with McDonald's, Microsoft, Wal-Mart, Best Buy, Bank of America, etc., then join them, by becoming shareholders, the preferred stocks is better. Then you own a stake in the business, and you will make money by letting those who know the industry best do the work.

Let's face it! Everyone is not called to own and manage their own business. However, we all can own and manage our wealth if our school system from day one would incorporate courses that would give students the proper teaching and training concerning money and investing for their future. Yes, our parents should help too, but they too are limited to what they themselves have been taught. And yes, we can and should continue to take greater responsibility in handling what we are earning now.

Oh, and the next time you hear one of those telemarketing commercials saying, *Are you tired of having to answer to a boss? Are you tired of them telling you when to be at work? Now you can start your own business! Just give us ex-amount of dollars and you can be in business for yourself today.*" Run for your pockets! I mean run for your lives! They are only interested in promoting their own business vision with your money; especially the ones where you are asked to go out and get others to buy into it too. They use you to do their advertising, why you buy their idea or products and then make you pay them for it in advance.

Trust me! These companies are not interested in your success, only your money. And surely you must know as well as they, if you are planning to have a successful business, you too will need to hire employees one day. Is that the attitude you want your employees to have concerning you? I think not!

> *Wealth from get-rich-quick schemes quickly disappears; wealth from hard work grows.*
> Proverbs 13:11 (NLT)

The Bible says that money answers every matter and that money is a defense. A defense that everyone should have! Then people will not need to lean upon social programs. Yes, I know some of these programs are necessary for those who really need them, like the elderly and the sick or disabled, but able-minded and able-bodied folks don't need them more than as a short-term vehicle to help get them back on their feet due to sickness or some form of hardship. Programs that are designed to keep one down or at a certain level in life are called the "Poverty Level Life."

> *For wisdom is a defense as money is a defense, but the excellence of knowledge is that wisdom gives life to those who have it.*
> Ecclesiastes 7:12 (NKJV)

> *A feast is made for laughter, and wine makes merry; but money answers everything.*
> Ecclesiastes 10:19 (NKJV)

During the year of 1990, after being open for three years, financial hardship struck. After struggling to pay everybody, I finally decided to move the business into my home. In fact I was so tired and stressed out, working day and night only to still come up short week after week, I just up and closed in one day. I rented a U-haul and moved everything into my home and worked from there. Things were so tight that one of my friends suggested I apply for welfare (food stamps and more). Though I may have qualified, I wouldn't do it because I felt that if I did, I might allow myself to become dependent upon it. I have seen this happen to several other people. They become complacent and begin to feel they can't do without it, or they are tempted to keep the assistance when it is no longer needed by coming up with deceitful ways to show they still need it.

There are indeed many people with physical or mental ailments who really need this assistance for the long term and some short term. However, there are thousands more who have allowed welfare to keep them from pursuing knowledge and skills because of deceit or laziness that otherwise could prosper them while meeting the needs of others. I thank the Lord for giving me a mind not to take that route, and I came through without having to rely on the welfare system.

> *Lazy people want much but get little, but those who work hard will prosper and be satisfied.*
> Proverbs 13:4 (NLT)

I've heard my pastor say many times, "*God doesn't want us to live on welfare all through life, but he wants us to fare well through life.*" He wants every generation to increase more and more, but he also wants us to have the knowledge and wisdom in how to increase and use those increases properly.

So many people struggle financially all through life, and when they are gone, they leave nothing to their loved ones they left behind. Sometimes they leave them more burdened after they are gone than when they were alive. The Lord wants us to leave blessings to our families, not curses. Through the mouth of King Solomon, he said a good man would not do that. Instead, he would leave an inheritance, financial and spiritual blessing, to his children and his grandchildren.

> *Good people leave an inheritance to their grandchildren, but the sinner's wealth passes to the godly.*
> Proverbs 13:22 (NLT)

Our history is full of nations that fell because they failed to teach and share the wealth and resources of the land; resources God put in the earth for each country to trade, buy, and sell. Knowledge is a seed to a good future, and so is money and other forms of resources.

If students were taught how they could have prosperous lifestyles through the power of wealth and the skills of their hands, I believe it would turn their focus off of all the sexual immorality. They would be too busy learning how to build lives rather than being destroyed. Teaching them how to have sex before they know how to build a family is totally out of order, and that is just what we have created—a generation out of order!

Teach them how to build wealth, and they will do that. Teach them how to kill, and they will do that. Teach them how to tell a lie, cheat, and steal, and they will do that. Teach them how to be unfaithful, and they will do that. The proof is in the pudding. Look around. Most of the things they are learning are negative and destructive, and these are the things many people do.

Teach children how to love and how to really live, and they will do that. We have to face it, folks! They are the cream of the crop. They are the produce from our seeds. They are the reaping from our sowing.

If the U.S. government were to offer free classes for all legal U.S. citizens who have gone through its school system so they can teach them this time the power of economics and how to truly create and build wealth instead of all these free programs, health care services, and classes to assist and teach the illegal immigrants to learn English and give them tax-exemption jobs and give us back what was wrongfully taken through excessive taxes, interest fees, late fees, over-limit fees, and, oh yes, doubling the punishment with penalty fees for being late on filing sales taxes and income taxes some business owners earn for them while struggling to survive, we would come back by the droves, just like the droves of illegal immigrants who flock into the U.S. every day for the free things our government offers and lets them get away with.

And don't get me wrong, I have nothing against people coming to the U.S. to build better lives for themselves and their families, because that is what God wants for all of us. If it was me and I saw a chance at a better life here, I would be trying to get here too. But there is a just way in which it should be done. I believe the Lord wants this to be a nation full of people from all nationalities under one God, the Lord Jesus Christ. Not only that, the Lord said to be careful how we treat foreigners because many of you were once foreigners, too.

> *Do not oppress foreigners in any way. Remember, you yourselves were once foreigners in the land of Egypt.*
> Exodus 22:21 (NLT)

I believe that if we had a system in place that would allow illegal immigrants to become legal citizens in a few weeks, rather than stretching the time for years through all the red tape mumble jumble, many of its own citizens could hire them legally to help us build a more prosperous and wealthy nation, instead of the ones who hire them illegally to build their own empires.

Why is it that it only takes a few minutes to pull up a credit report and know your history for at least ten years or more, then draw up documents to cut you a loan for a house or a business, have them signed and delivered in just a matter of minutes, and your property built in just a few weeks or months, yet it takes years to make one human being a legal member of a state? I just don't get it. Then again, I guess I really do. It's called hog wash, red tape, and bureaucracy!

> *If you see a poor person being oppressed by the powerful and justice being miscarried throughout the land, don't be surprised! For every official is under orders from higher up, and matters of justice only get lost in red tape and bureaucracy. Even the king milks the land for his own profit!*
>
> Ecclesiastes 5:8–9 (NLT)

> *One day Jesus told his disciples a story to illustrate their need for constant prayer and to show them that they must never give up. "There was a judge in a certain city," he said, "who was a godless man with great contempt for everyone. A widow of that city came to him repeatedly, appealing for justice against someone who had harmed her. The judge ignored her for a while, but eventually she wore him out. 'I fear neither God nor man,' he said to himself, 'but this woman is driving me crazy. I'm going to see that she gets justice, because she is wearing me out with her constant requests!' "Then the Lord said, "Learn a lesson from this evil judge. Even he rendered a just decision in the end, so don't you think God will surely give justice to his chosen people who plead with him day and night? Will he keep putting them off? I tell you, he will grant justice to them quickly! But when I, the Son of Man, return, how many will I find who have faith?"*
>
> Luke 18:1–8 (NLT)

It's like King Solomon said, "There is nothing new under the sun." There were unjust judges in Jesus' day, and they are still here today.

The passage above proves that there will always be unjust people in the world, but the Lord God of justice and mercy, sees it all. No one gets away with anything! Not even sweet little ole me! So repent and make things right with God and he will forgive you. And don't worry about those who have wronged you. He will see to it that those who fear him are avenged. The Judge of all judges is on the way. Yip-pie! In the meantime, hang tight until he performs it for you, at the appointed time.

Let the field be joyful, and all that is in it. Then all the trees of the woods will rejoice before the Lord. For He is coming, for He is coming to judge the earth. He shall judge the world with righteousness, and the peoples with His truth.
Psalms 96:12–13 (NKJV)

Knowledge and wisdom are definitely the keys to life and the expansion of it in every area, whether pursuing to be a teacher, an artist, a judge, etc. Wisdom and knowledge are even far greater needed in the area of one's finances. It helps us to maintain and increase what we gain from our skills and talents. Financial literacy would greatly decrease over 50 percent of the debt problems we have in this country and maybe even eradicate them all together. After all, knowledge empowers people to conquer whatever is trying to destroy them. Ask any military officer that, and I bet you they will say, "When we were given the right strategic plan and equipped ourselves with strength to fight to the end, then we win the war."

Winning a battle is not easy, and we all need to win the war on debt and financial illiteracy in our country. The United States of America needs a new strategy in her school system that will teach her students how to conquer and win in life and in the world.

Financial literacy will help people to be in control of their own destinies. Learning how to handle money wisely should be taught at home too. However, because many parents in the home have not been taught to manage and invest money, many are unable to teach their children successfully.

So the debt problem of our nation increases more and more with each generation. Debt in itself is not destructive, but the misuse of it is, and that comes from not being properly taught how to use it. As a result, it robs us of our time, life, and even our family's future. And it is very expensive just to be alive these days, even the unborn need lawyers to defend their right to life.

> *About this time some of the men and their wives raised a cry of protest against their fellow Jews. They were saying, "We have such large families. We need more money just so we can buy the food we need to survive." Others said, "We have mortgaged our fields, vineyards, and homes to get food during the famine." And others said, "We have already borrowed to the limit on our fields and vineyards to pay our taxes. We belong to the same family, and our children are just like theirs. Yet we must sell our children into slavery just to get enough money to live. We have already sold some of our daughters, and we are helpless to do anything about it, for our fields and vineyards are already mortgaged to others."*
>
> Nehemiah 5:1–5 (NLT)

This problem of debt is nothing new, as you can see. It has been used down through the years to oppress people, families, and nations. Debt here in the United States goes back as far as 1791. When the Federal Reserve came on the scene, it was 1913.

We are to train children in the way they are to go, and that includes money management and investing as well as spirituality and sexuality, etc. The Word of God teaches more about money than any other subject in the Bible, and we should too. Money is mentioned in every book of the Bible from Genesis to Revelation. Money is the number-one tool necessary for one to function in the world system. You will earn it or you will steal it because you can't live without it. It is a vital part of every life.

> *The wealth of the rich is their fortress; the poverty of the poor is their calamity.*
>
> Proverbs 10:15 (NLT)

How can you increase in wealth if you were not taught how? And how can you leave it for your children if you don't have it to leave? The principles of money should be taught from the moment a child says, "Give me some money!" In other words, "Okay, you want some money, then let me teach you first of all what it is, its purpose, how to obtain it, and make it multiply!" From childhood, we should be taught how to master it so it will not master us. They should know the Lord wants them to prosper, but not to put their trust in their wealth, only in the Lord. The Lord teaches us and we are to teach them. Remember, every generation is a reflection of the one before it. If they don't learn it in school and at home, the generations after them won't know it either.

> *Thus saith the Lord, thy Redeemer, the Holy One of Israel; I am the Lord thy God which teacheth thee to profit, which leadeth thee by the way that thou shouldest go.*
> *Isaiah 48:17 (KJV)*

> *Train up a child in the way he should go: and when he is old, he will not depart from it.*
> *Proverbs 22:6 (KJV)*

> *Trust in your money and down you go! But the godly flourish like leaves in spring.*
> *Proverbs 11:28 (NLT)*

The more I began to study investing in the stock market and other paths to financial stability, the more it grieved me to see how far behind I was, yet pushing every day to get ahead. It is hard to get ahead if you are not taught ahead of time the principles of sound investing and how to increase wealth and maintain it. But thank God, I am learning. Now I'm waiting and watching for what I'm learning and have begun to apply, to catch up with me and thrust me ahead.

Money is definitely both a tool and a weapon to help you provide and protect the needs of your family and others as well as support the Kingdom of God. The Lord uses it and other resources as a tool to test our heart and build character in us. It is like a gauge that measures and reveals the character of a person, a corporation, and a government. It's true a person's checkbook or credit statements will tell where their heart and priorities are. It is equally true about a company and a government. Where the tax dollars or a corporation's donations or campaign dollars go, show where their hearts are.

> *Wherever your treasure is, there your heart and thoughts will also be.*
>
> Matthew 6:21 (NLT)

Based on the things I have learned in life thus far, if I could start my life all over, I would make these studies in life my top priority—finances and economics, because it teaches you how to increase and live financially free; I would pursue my youthful dream of being an Architect, right along with Tailoring, because they both go hand in hand. Both are capable of creating an original blueprint in order to produce the find project. And I would continue to study the word of God, because it teaches me how to love and to wisely profit in life. It teaches us how not to be like a fool with his money, and most of all, how to live and be eternally free. More importantly, I find the best investments one can ever make, is in their relationship with the Lord, their spouse and children, souls for eternity and don't forget, the stock market.

> *"After a long time their master returned from his trip and called them to give an account of how they had used his*

money. The servant to whom he had entrusted the five bags of gold said, 'Sir, you gave me five bags of gold to invest, and I have doubled the amount.' The master was full of praise. 'Well done, my good and faithful servant. You have been faithful in handling this small amount, so now I will give you many more responsibilities. Let's celebrate together!'

Next came the servant who had received two bags of gold, 'Sir, you gave me two bags of gold to invest, and I have doubled the amount. The master said, "Well done, my good and faithful servant. You have been faithful in handling this small amount, so now I will give you many more responsibilities. Let's celebrate together!"

"Then the servant with the one bag of gold came and said, 'Sir, I know you are a hard man, harvesting crops you didn't plant and gathering crops you didn't cultivate. I was afraid I would lose your money, so I hid it in the earth and here it is.' "But the master replied, 'You wicked and lazy servant! You think I'm a hard man, do you, harvesting crops I didn't plant and gathering crops I didn't cultivate? Well, you should at least have put my money into the bank so I could have some interest.

Matthew 25:19–28(NLT)

Happy is person who finds wisdom and gains understanding. For the profit of wisdom is better than silver, and her wages are better than gold.

Proverbs 3:13–14(NLT)

The fruit of the righteous is a tree of life, And he who wins souls is wise.

Proverbs 11:30 (NKJV)

But thou shalt remember the L<small>ORD</small> thy God: for it is he that giveth thee power to get wealth, that he may establish his covenant which he sware unto thy fathers, as it is this day.

Deuteronomy 8:18(KJV)

God Is In Charge

All the ends of the world shall remember and turn unto the LORD: and all the kindreds of the nations shall worship before thee. For the kingdom is the LORD's: and he is the governor among the nations.
Psalm 22:27-28 (NKJV)

God is "The" Commander in Chief of the Armies of Heavens. He is also called "The Lord of Host" and "Man of War." He is the one who gives victory in battle. Several times when the children of Israel's enemies attacked them, the Lord had given their kings and leaders strategic plans on how to defeat them. All through the Old Covenant, you see where the Lord himself fought for his people. He fought Israel's enemies in their first war and He is going to fight their enemies in their last war. Several times he sent an angel or angels to fight for them.

And it came to pass, when Joshua was by Jericho, that he lifted his eyes and looked, and behold, a Man stood opposite him with

> *His sword drawn in His hand. And Joshua went to Him and said to Him, "Are You for us or for our adversaries?"*
>
> *So He said, "No, but as Commander of the army of the LORD I have now come."*
>
> *And Joshua fell on his face to the earth and worshiped, and said to Him, "What does my Lord say to His servant?" Then the Commander of the LORD's army said to Joshua, "Take your sandal off your foot, for the place where you stand is holy." And Joshua did so.*
>
> Joshua 5:13–15 (NKJV)

There are no armies like the armies of the Lord God. The armies of the earth are no match for the armies of heaven. One day the king of Aram sent his armies of horses and chariots after Elisha, a prophet of God. They had no idea the armies of the God Most High would surround them. When they pursued the prophet of God, they were pursuing God. So the Lord dispatched his armies of horses and chariots of fire to protect Elisha and his servant.

> *So one night the king of Aram sent a great army with many chariots and horses to surround the city. When the servant of the man of God got up early the next morning and went outside, there were troops, horses, and chariots everywhere.*
>
> *"Ah, my lord, what will we do now?" he cried out to Elisha. "Don't be afraid!" Elisha told him. "For there are more on our side than on theirs!" Then Elisha prayed, "O LORD, open his eyes and let him see!" The LORD opened his servant's eyes, and when he looked up, he saw that the hillside around Elisha was filled with horses and chariots of fire.*
>
> 2 Kings 6:14–17 (NLT)

Oh, if only we had leaders who are keenly aware of this and would remember to call on the Lord of Host, especially in times of war, to instruct them on if and when they should go to war, and for a strategic plan of action that would bring victory and a quick end.

The Lord is our Creator. He is God of the whole earth, everyone on it and everything beneath it. The earth is like one big kingdom with millions of living quarters and rooms and lots of family members of all ages and talents. He is a wonderful father and provider. He provided acres and acres of land for his huge earthly kingdom and family, so they may multiply and flourish throughout all the earth. The land around the property is designed with lots of lustrous parks and streams of rivers that are just as beautiful as the Garden of Eden. Birds and animals browse the grounds round about his family. High above these acres of land, too far for the human eye or a telescope to see, sit his office, the Most High Place. His Servants he called Angels and Ministers of Flaming of Fire.

> *Then Micaiah continued, "Listen to what the LORD says! I saw the LORD sitting on his throne with all the armies of heaven around him, on his right and on his left.*
> 1 Kings 22:19(NLT)

These Angelic Ministers are like Law-keepers, Bodyguards, Landscapers and Gatekeepers appointed to oversee God's huge earthly family. These Angelic beings are appointed to every member of his family. They are appointed to guard them and minister to them with blessings. They greatly reverence God with awe and wonder. Each one of them understands their roles perfectly and they oversee everything with fear and reverence. They stand strong and mighty in his presence ready to carry out all his orders. They minister to God's family everything he has provided according as he commands and according to the family member's obedience.

One day, one of the Angelic beings name Lucifer (Satan), rebelled and made war in heaven and he was permanently removed from his position. He caused a third of the Angelic hosts to rebel with him and they too were all permanently removed from their position. They were once keepers of truth and light, but now they are keepers of deception and darkness. Now the others have an even greater task of being the Armed Forces. Not only do they have the role to oversee the family of God on earth, they also have to stand and fight against these rebels who once stood with them. But when the appointed time comes, these rebels will be put away permanently for rebelling against God.

> *And war broke out in heaven: Michael and his angels fought with the dragon; and the dragon and his angels fought, but they did not prevail, nor was a place found for them in heaven any longer. So the great dragon was cast out, that serpent of old, called the Devil and Satan, who deceives the whole world; he was cast to the earth, and his angels were cast out with him.*
>
> Revelation 12:7–9(NKJV)

> *The devil, who deceived them, was cast into the lake of fire and brimstone where the beast and the false prophet are. And they will be tormented day and night forever and ever.*
>
> Revelation 20:10(NKJV)

Two thirds of these Mighty Angelic Keepers still stands serving the Lord God. They are constantly on guard to keep the enemy from taking and devouring what the Father has provided for his family. They are on guard at all times, ready to carry out the orders of their Commander in Chief. They never argue or rebel against his word, because they recognize and reverence his holy authority and righteousness. When he speaks they move.

> Then the LORD thundered, "Bring on the men appointed to punish the city! Tell them to bring their weapons with them!" Six men soon appeared from the upper gate that faces north, each carrying a battle club in his hand. One of them was dressed in linen and carried a writer's case strapped to his side. They all went into the Temple courtyard and stood beside the bronze altar. And the LORD called to the man dressed in linen who was carrying the writer's case. He said to him, "Walk through the streets of Jerusalem and put a mark on the foreheads of all those who weep and sigh because of the sins they see around them." Then I heard the LORD say to the other men, "Follow him through the city and kill everyone whose forehead is not marked. Show no mercy; have no pity!
>
> Ezekiel 9:1–5 (NLT)

> Then the man in linen clothing, who carried the writer's case, reported back and said, "I have finished the work you gave me to do."
>
> Ezekiel 9:11 (NLT)

This passage above is an event that will take place sometime in the future doing the Great Tribulation period. You see God wants us to know the things that are to come. The word of God is not just about the God of the past, but it's about God and human history, past, present and future, and how he deals with mankind as an individual and as a nation.

God is also a great father. He is a parent to all who has accepted Jesus, his son. And like God is a parent, so leaders of nations, states, cities, companies and the churches like parents. The President is like the father of the house and he is the Commander in Chief. Like the positions of the Angels, so are the Armed Forces, Congressional Members, Judges, and the other departments of government, such as, the Department of Agriculture, Energy, Commerce, Labor, Defense, Transportation, Homeland Security and etc. They are appointed as the overseers of the families of the nation's resources and services. They are Housekeepers of the provision, the Landscapers of the land, the Gatekeepers of the law and the Armed Forces of our land, sky and seas. These individuals are appointed to oversee the domestic and international concerns of the nation's house and its citizens in order that the law of the land and the will of the President and Commander in Chief are also carried out. They are appointed to carry out the constitution given by the fathers of the nation. But like the Angelic beings who rebelled against the will of God, some of the leaders argue and rebel against the authority and will of God and the forefathers.

Some of them have become greedy and corrupted and have lost sight of their position and therefore they abuse it. They accept bribes for special favors and some even sell out the nation's sovereignty. This is because the Angelic Servants that rebel against the will of the God of the heavens now influences these leaders to rebel against his will for the families of the earth. Many of them have an agenda to keep us from reaching our God's appointed destiny, but they fail to realize, God is in charge. He has a higher agenda. And there is no plan known unto man that can outweigh or overthrow the plan of God. Nor will there ever be one. Those who counsel against the will of the Lord will not succeed.

The LORD shatters the plans of the nations and thwarts all their schemes. But the LORD's plans stand firm forever; his intentions can never be shaken.
Psalm 33:10–11 (NLT)

You can make many plans, but the LORD's purpose will prevail.
Proverbs 19:21 (NLT)

Everything about our lives mimics the kingdom of light or the kingdom of darkness. Whether positions in high places of authority such as presidents, scholars and dignitaries, to a common blue collar worker. Though people lose their way or get out of their roles, that doesn't keep God from being who he is or doing what he has planned.

God is always in control. He watches everything that takes place here on earth. Even when the leaders of nations get off track, the Lord will still fulfill his will and he will help us fulfill our destiny. Maybe the Lord has appointed some of you to fill a position in our government and help put the United States back on the right course. Whatever the case maybe, you are called to serve in the arena of life.

Most High God rules the kingdoms of the world and appoints anyone he desires to rule over them.
Daniel 5:21b (NLT)

John replied, "God in heaven appoints each person's work."
John 3:27 (NLT)

Redeem the Time

Everything has already been decided. It was known long ago what each person would be. So there's no use arguing with God about your destiny.
                                            Ecclesiastes 6:10 (NLT)

Parents ask your teens, what is it that they really wanted to accomplish in life. Some of you would be surprised at their answers. No matter how strange or unreasonable it may sound, it's worth you finding out and certainly worth achieving if it is God's will for them. Whatever the Lord has created us for he's already equipped us for it. If your children are grown and still don't know their purpose in life, that is partly your fault, but it is not too late to help them or you to seek the Lord on the matter. Moreover, by the time a person reaches adulthood, they should have a hunger to know their purpose in life, if they are not already living it. If this is you, ask the Lord for guidance and all the assistance needed in order to accomplish it. The Lord has not forgotten you. Maybe some of you have forgotten him. It was decided long ago, what you and your children were to be, so don't argue with God about your destiny. He has the best plan, so ask him and get moving. First and foremost, be sure you have prayed the prayer of salvation. Make sure above all things that your sins are forgiven, through faith and confession in God's son Christ Jesus. Your being reconciled back to God through Jesus Christ is God's ultimate plan for all humanity. If you have not accepted the Lord Jesus, as Lord and Savior, please pray the prayer of salvation at the end of the book and you will become a brand new person inside (a born again spirit); a brand new start; a loving relationship with the true and living God and the gift of eternal life.

> *For the wages of sin is death, but the free gift of God is eternal life through Christ Jesus our Lord.*
> *Romans 6:23 (NLT)*

> *And this is what God has testified: He has given us eternal life, and this life is in his Son. So whoever has God's Son has life; whoever does not have his Son does not have life.*
> *I John 5:11–13 (NLT)*

> *And this is the way to have eternal life—to know you, the only true God, and Jesus Christ, the one you sent to earth.*
> *John 17:3 (NLT)*

Read your Bible so that you can really know the Lord Jesus Christ. Build yourself up in the word of God through prayer and Bible study. It is crucial that you read the word of God so that you may know the Truth and be able to recognize the spirit of falsehood and the Antichrist. The word of God reveals the past, the present and the things to come and no psychic in the world can do that. In fact the word of God exposes them to you too and the evil spirits behind them.

> *For example, never sacrifice your son or daughter as a burnt offering. And do not let your people practice fortune-telling or sorcery, or allow them to interpret omens, or engage in witchcraft, or cast spells, or function as mediums or psychics, or call forth the spirits of the dead. Anyone who does these things is an object of horror and disgust to the LORD. It is because the other nations have done these things that the LORD your God will drive them out ahead of you. You must be blameless before the LORD your God.*
> Deuteronomy 18:10–13(NLT)

The word of God is Truth and Light. It covers every issue concerning life and reveals to us the events to come. The Lord does not want us in the dark about anything. That's why he has given us his Spirit and his word. Reading the Bible will cause you to renew your mind so you will see things as the Lord God does and not as those who opposes him. As you do this your life will constantly be renewed and take on a whole new meaning and purpose. And no matter what trials come your way, keep your chin up and your knees bowed. Pour out your heart to God and let him know how you feel about everything.

Read the word of God daily and ask him to show you how to apply it in your life. Then watch your life began to shape up, while sinful behaviors and negative things began to ship out. Most people say start reading the book of John in the New Testament, which is a great place to start. It would be even better to ask the Lord to reveal to you where he would have you to start reading first. If you still are not clear on it, start with the book of John. Also, ask the Lord to show you the church he wants you to attend for your spiritual growth. It is important that you ask the Lord to guide you, because not all church leaders speak and teach the truth of God's word with a reverential fear and knowledge of God. Ask him and he will certainly show you where you need to be. And remember, there is *nothing* too hard for God. He controls our destiny, because he is the God of all destinies and he is Lord and King of everything. Let go of the past, the anger, the bitterness, and even forgive yourself and move on. Your destiny is waiting for you.

> *Then I realized how bitter I had become, how pained I had been by all I had seen. I was so foolish and ignorant—I must have seemed like a senseless animal to you. Yet I still belong to you; you are holding my right hand. You will keep on guiding me with your counsel, leading me to a glorious destiny. Whom have I in heaven but you? I desire you more than anything on earth. My health may fail, and my spirit may grow weak, but God remains the strength of my heart; he is mine forever.*
> Psalms 73:21–26 (NLT)

Life, indeed, is a journey full of trials, pain, suffering, and afflictions, as well as the good things we all encounter. It seems we walk out of one trial, only to find another one waiting for us. Sometimes they are caused by our own doing. Often they catch us by surprise, but nothing catches God by surprise. He saw it coming and sometimes he sends them. Trials test our faith and sadness has a way of refining us. Our faith is like a precious commodity. It's worth more than pure gold, so is our faith and our lives to the Lord. When trials come, our faith is being tested to see if it is strong and pure, but sometimes we fail to recognize it.

I heard a gentleman say once, "Everything that comes into our lives is either God sent or God used." Nothing is wasted, and nothing in the life of a believer is a coincidence. Everything we encounter in our lives has a reason. No matter what your pain or sorrow, or whatever you have gone through, or going through now, God notices it. Whatever the circumstances may be, the Lord still has a plan. Sometimes the Lord allows things and situations to happen in our lives to bring about something wonderful in us, for us, or through us; Sometimes, to bring about judgment or correction, in a person, a city, or a nation. Let's face it! None of us are good all the time.

> *For the LORD corrects those he loves, just as a father corrects a child in whom he delights.*
> Proverbs 3:12 (NLT)

The Lord uses trials as an opportunity to display his love and power. Jesus and his disciples came upon a blind man one day and his disciples asked him why he was born blind. They thought it was because of his sins or his parents' sins. But Jesus said neither and explained why.

> *As Jesus was walking along, he saw a man who had been blind from birth. "Teacher," his disciples asked him, "why was this man born blind? Was it a result of his own sins or those of his parents?" "It was not because of his sins or his parents' sins," Jesus answered. "He was born blind so the power of God could be seen in him.*
> John 9:1–4 (NLT)

Then Jesus said this to them:

> *All of us must quickly carry out the tasks assigned us by the one who sent me, because there is little time left before the night falls and all work comes to an end.*
> John 9:4 (NLT)

You see, we all have been sent here with a task to do. Jesus revealed to his disciples and to us, that though we do not see or understand the whole scope of God, he has a purpose for everyone and in everything.

Since our Creator has already designed our life's blueprint. We never have to be in the dark concerning his plans. So Put down your boxing gloves and pick up the word of God. Don't argue with him about your destiny. He knows and wants what is best for us. And no matter what trials life may bring, he is in control of our lives and dreams. The Lord didn't say how far we would go in life. That is up to us. His word says, *It was determined long ago what each person were to be in life.* So do the best you can. It's not too late. And it's in you to succeed.

Now, when all is said and done, what will your life's report read? Unknown! Incomplete! Or Mission Accomplished! Either way, you choose. Remember, God is still in charge and he's for you. Though our trials seem to trample us down, trials don't last. And like lemons lead to lemonade and mistakes lead to miracles, so do trials lead to triumph!

> *Because the Sovereign LORD helps me, I will not be dismayed. Therefore, I have set my face like a stone, determined to do his will. And I know that I will triumph.*
>
> Isaiah 50:7 (NLT)

Prayer for Salvation

God of all creation;
Of the heavens, the earth and everything
that dwells upon it and beneath it.
I want to be born again.
You said if I call upon the name of Jesus, I shall be saved.
Forgive me of my sins and save me.
I believe you sent Jesus, your Beloved Son, to die for my sins.
I believe that you raised Jesus from the dead.
Jesus, I want you to be my Lord and Savior
and grant me the Gift of Eternal Life.
Heavenly Father, I ask this in the name
of Jesus, your only begotten Son;
Who at this moment is now become
my Savior, Lord and King;
And has now given me the Gift of Eternal Life,
according to Roman 10:9–13.
Thank you that my name is written
in the Lamb's Book of Life
according to Revelation 21:27.
Heaven Father,
Sanctify me in your word and teach me
your truth through the Holy Spirit
according to your word in John 16:13–14 and John 17:17.
Teach me to know your ways and fulfill your plan for my life.
Thank you Heavenly Father, In Jesus name, Amen.

God's Appointed Destiny (GAD)

I have written four other books in connection to "GAD." They are simply waiting to be polished and published. These books cover things many of us need and want to know. Some of the subject titles and discussions are:

1. Destiny Hidden in a Name
   Cities Destined According to its Name
   Face to Face with the Lord of Destines
   The Great Decoder
   When Shalom Entered My Life
   When Taishan Arrived

2. Who Can Find A Faithful Man
   A Call To Loyalty
   Meant to Complement
   Real Jewels

If Men are So Visual, What are We? Blind?
Another Perfect Match?
It's Your Thing, Do What You Wanna Do!
When the Girls Go Bob-Bob Bobbin Along
It Takes Two Baby
Drunk on Sexual Immorality
Tell Victoria the Secret Is Out

1. What Man Rejects, God Selects
   Trials Lead To Triumph
   Prison Bars Can't Stop the Plan of God
   The King and I
   Your Mouth Or Your Life
   Awake From Thy Stupor
   What God Reveals, God Fulfills
   Mission Accomplished

2. The World's Greatest Investor and Mentor
   Religion or Relationship
   The Last Subpoena
   The Last Trump
   One Devil Don't Stop No Show
   Global Warming or Hell Making Room?

I have also written a prayer book for leaders, one for teens and one for children. Please stay tuned for upcoming books and their release dates and other offers. I would also love to receive your comments and book reviews concerning this book. So please send your email to **gad4you@aol.com**. You can also visit my website at **www.GADseries.com**.

Thank you for supporting me and reading my book. I hope you have been edified and motivated to seek the Lord more and to finish your course in life too. God bless you.

ALSO AVAILABLE FOR THIS TITLE:

Audio Book Digital Download
Audio Book Product
eBook Digital Download

Once downloaded to your computer, you can listen to the book through your computer's speakers, burn it to an audio CD or save the file to your portable music device (such as Apple's popular iPod) and listen on the go!

The eBook is also convenient for people on the go- and handy for popular eBook readers.

Prices vary according to item. Visit www.tatepublishing.com/bookstore for more information.